Brush *with*
Haiti

Brush *with*

Haiti

KATHLEEN A. TOBIN

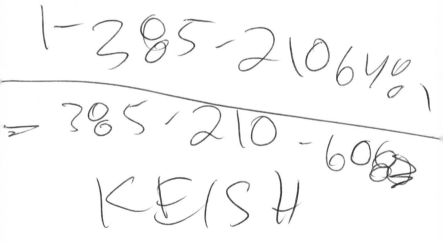

1-385-21064

= 385-210-606

KEISH

MILL CITY PRESS

Minneapolis

Mill City Press, Inc.
212 3rd Avenue North, Suite 290
Minneapolis, MN 55401
612.455.2294
www.millcitypublishing.com

ISBN-13: 978-1-938223-85-3
LCCN: 2012920064

Book Design by Kristeen Ott

Printed in the United States of America

To university students everywhere

1
SHOCK

There is nothing much to remember about the landing at O'Hare, except it was sometime around 4:30 or so on January 12th. I had not spoken much to the people near me on the flight. I rarely do, except for a bit of small talk here and there. As we taxied to the gate, I turned on my cell phone.

I saw there was a message from my daughter. Before listening to it, I called to see what was up. My kids don't keep track of my schedule – nor do I keep track of my mother's – so Katie timing a call so perfectly in order to welcome me home from Port-au-Prince was unlikely. Perhaps something was up in her life, requiring a long-distance shoulder to lean on. In the center of the plane, amid passengers scrambling to gather their belongings, I waited for her to pick up. When she did, I could not understand a word she was saying. She was hysterical. Her sobs were not completely unfamiliar but she had been on her own in Nashville for some time, and things seemed to be going so well.

"Mom!" she cried into the phone. I looked at the travelers around me to see whether they were hearing the other side of this conversation. It was nearly deafening to me. I wondered how I could possibly do anything to help her from Chicago. She went on, incoherently.

"Katie, take a breath. I can't understand what you're saying." She went on, apparently repeating herself, but I still could not decipher anything. "Slow down."

"Wah, blah… something, something… earthquake!" is what I heard. Oh, my God, I thought. An earthquake in Tennessee? That didn't seem possible. I prayed she wasn't hurt.

"Mom, are you ok?"

"Yes, are you ok?" I needed to be sure.

"Yes! Are YOU ok?"

"I'm fine!" I assured her in a voice more stern than necessary. She was making absolutely no sense to me.

"Mom, where are you?" she asked. I wondered how fast I could get to Nashville.

"I'm at O'Hare. Our plane just landed."

"You're safe? There was an earthquake in Haiti!"

What? She must have meant hurricane. There are no earthquakes in Haiti, I thought. But the urgency in her voice was not a hurricane kind of urgency.

"Mom, there was terrible earthquake in Port-au-Prince! They're saying it was a 7.9 or something!"

"Oh, my God." I slumped back in my seat. I had friends in California and had developed some Richter scale sensitivities. If an earthquake of this magnitude truly hit Port-au-Prince the city would be devastated. Memories of the little girls in their freshly ironed uniforms trotting off to school in the sunshine just hours before flooded my mind. I turned to the others in my row.

"There was an earthquake in Haiti, and I just came from there." I told her I would call her back.

I sat numb while passengers took their bags from overhead compartments, and when it was my turn, stood into a film of detachment. At some point following, my friend Renate and I spoke. I don't remember if I called her or she called me, nor whether it was at the baggage claim or beyond. And I don't remember much of the conversation past the first words.

"Did you hear?" she asked.

"I heard." It was impossible to know what to say. She had left Port-au-Prince on a flight following mine, and was at the airport in Miami.

Renate had lived in Haiti for six years, working in various areas of health care and education, primarily in the Grand'Anse region on the southwest peninsula. She also had many friends in Port-au-Prince. I had contacted her not quite a year before, following a nasty spell at work, to see if she might help me arrange a brief research visit. On the wrong side of university politics – in retrospect on the right side – I needed a reality check to clear my head. Visiting some area of the developing world always provided that for me.

I considered myself fortunate in teaching Latin American history. It gave me a sense of balance and perspective and trips to El Salvador, Guatemala, and so on – no matter how brief – lent themselves to nurturing a sense of inner calm, and served to remind me of life's priorities. I knew I risked setting myself apart at work even more by going away for a while, but the egos, deception, and power mongering of university politics had gotten under my skin. Way too deep under my skin. It was time for a cleansing.

I had visited Haiti once before, and knew Renate might arrange for me to meet with people in education, just to talk. I had considered a curriculum sharing project, or some such thing, but decided first to investigate teaching methods and schooling structures there. To be honest, I was not sure exactly what it was I wanted to do, or what might come of it. She said she would contact some people and get back to me. At that point she was returning to Chicago, as grant money for her current project was running out, but planned to get back to Haiti in late December and said she could meet me there.

She was able to put me in touch with teachers and school directors, and the trip fit nicely into winter break. I met her in Jeremie, the seat of the Department of the Grand'Anse. After several days there, we flew back to Port-au-Prince where we continued our work separately. On January 12th, I flew out in the late morning and she in the afternoon. Hers was the last flight out.

Dazed, I walked through the O'Hare terminal and looked for a news broadcast. Television sets dotted the waiting areas, and they all carried the story. It was apparently true. But there were no cameras in Port-au-Prince yet, so the reports resorted to maps and graphics. Perhaps there was a chance it was not true, I prayed. A mistake. A false report. A news rumor gone wild. I watched the lounging travelers staring at the televisions. They seemed to believe it.

There is always a bit of reality warp when entering the U.S. after a visit to an underdeveloped country, a feeling that Americans have no real understanding of the human condition. The plane ride exists as a sort of nebulous place between two worlds, a vacuum in which one decompresses before entering the sanitized realm of material consumption plastered against a backdrop of non-descript music. In the unreal world of the airport, the story of an earthquake in an already struggling metropolis seemed impossible.

But it wasn't. I collected my bags and meandered through the ground level to the suburban-bound bus area. It seemed as far from the center of reality as one could imagine. There was no television set there. I put on the extra long-sleeved t-shirt that had been stuffed into the bottom of my purse and the lightweight trench coat which I had tied around my waist. More than a foot of snow had fallen while I was away, and the early darkness of winter made the cold air even colder. The next bus was not due for another 45 minutes. I found an empty seat among the black vinyl and chrome bench and sat down. Then I began to cry. And cry. The young man seated across from me looked up and then down at his hands. I imagined he thought it was love troubles or something.

Once on the bus, I rested my head against the window. Those rides are always silent, except when the driver stops to collect tickets or announce a transfer. Even when couples or family members chat on their way home from wherever they happened to be their voices are muffled and seem distant. The film of detachment that had fallen down around me with my daughter's call remained, keeping me from understanding anything.

As we reached the bus station, I wrapped my thin coat tighter around me, grabbed the handles of my suitcases, and dragged them to the car. The wheels were rendered useless, and my shoes filled with snow. The evening before, I had stood on my balcony in Port-au-Prince watching the sunset and preparing myself mentally for the return to a frigid Chicago. And now, even without gloves or a hat, I felt nothing. I unlocked my car and it started up without hesitating. As the engine warmed, I stepped out and brushed the snow from the front and back windows with my bare hands. There. Good enough, I told myself. Driving after being away is a bit surreal anyway, and not having a perfectly full view would intensify that.

I turned on WXRT, a gratifyingly authentic Chicago radio station, to help bring my mind back home. Before I left the parking lot, my phone rang again. It was my mother.

"Are you hungry?" she asked. "I made some extra dinner and we're watching CNN." I was famished and did not want to go home to an empty house and an even emptier refrigerator. And I wanted to see a television, more than ever before in my life.

That night my parents' house felt the best of all possible places to be. It was warm and bright and smelled of Tuesday dinner. I sat down on the sofa and my mother brought me plates and plates of food. Apparently it was her expression of gratitude for the fact that I made it home safely. My father and sister were there, too, and seemed equally grateful to be with me. I was not sure what to say. I stared at the television and my eyes welled up with tears.

"I don't think I've ever seen the word 'Haiti' on television before," I told my dad. The country had experienced turmoil before, but my brain's memory functions were not operational. Before I had left on the trip, I wondered whether it was necessary to leave a detailed itinerary with anyone. Renate convinced me to do so, but the task only made me realize what a strange situation I had lived myself into. Divorced for eight years and not in a serious relationship, there was no significant other to play the role of contact should there be some sort of emergency.

Katie was 25-years-old, and might well have been growing into the best choice, but she was living in Nashville. My 21-year-old son, Dan, was away at Case Western Reserve in Cleveland and living in a fraternity house, and… well that would not do. My father was frail and aging quickly, and to be honest, my mother would not be much help at all in an international disaster situation. I asked one of my sisters who lived close by if I could leave the itinerary with her, just in case anything happened.

"Can't someone else be in charge of that?" she asked.

"Oh, come on. Nothing's going to happen," I replied. I knew she was busy and all, but jeez. Seriously. I must have caught her at a bad time, or maybe just by surprise because I had never asked such a thing before.

Sam, my 17-year-old, seemed the only choice. But he was still my baby. How could it possibly be that my baby would have to be designated as the one to bail me out of a problem? He would let his father know if anything happened, I thought, who surely would have had the wherewithal to do something useful. Or not.

Never before in my life was I much concerned with keeping someone informed of my whereabouts, and I am not sure why I was this time. After the fact, a friend suggested I might have had a premonition. But I don't think so. It was just a new awareness that I had succeeded so well in my quest for independence that perhaps no one would know if something were to happen to me. In any case, the close call was also a wake-up call, and it seemed to bring everyone nearer. And from my mother came more plates of food. Watching the news unfold, even without actual footage from the country, I realized I was not really hungry at all.

The difficult days following the earthquake turned into weeks. More people than I could imagine wanted to talk about it, and I had so little to say. It was hard to make sense of why anyone would want my take on it. People were suffering. And I wasn't there. That was it.

As the weeks turned into months, I began piecing together what I had come to know about the country, and how I came to know it. I found a delicate balance between the processes by which Haiti came into my life and of my active pursuit to learn more. And through it, I came to remember the passion I once held, and the realization of how little I knew at all.

2
FIRST CLASS

The first time I taught anything about Haiti was in the spring of 1995, as part of a Modern Latin America history class at Valparaiso University. I had successfully defended my Ph.D. dissertation at the University of Chicago the summer before, and was still on the "adjunct circuit" alternating courses at any of three campuses near my home in northwest Indiana. My children were young and my husband secure in an English teaching job at local high school, which he did not want to leave. Teaching U.S. History surveys was satisfying enough, but I actively kept my eyes open for other opportunities.

In the first week of classes during the previous semester, a professor teaching a course on the American Revolution had suffered a severe heart attack and a colleague at one of my other campuses mentioned in a department meeting that they were looking for a replacement. I called the Valparaiso history department that afternoon. Such circumstances help to give academia a reputation for being heartless, and it is a bit horrifying to admit I found myself taking advantage of the situation. But the students needed an instructor, and the class turned out to be a success.

While I was there, I learned they were looking for someone to cover a Latin American History course the following semester. It seemed their Latin Americanist had died a few years earlier and they had not replaced him. This was an even worse set of circumstances. In the other case, I could at least convince myself I might be helping in the professor's recovery by relieving him of the worry surrounding his American Revolution class. But this guy was dead. Perhaps it is the academic historian in me who sees life and death as something wholly common and inevitable and that is what gave me the courage to volunteer. After all, our work centers on the lives of dead people. It is not as if any individual's life or death is inevitable. How they play out depends upon a myriad of conditions and choices. But people do come and go; even history professors. And I heard he did a wonderful job and had left a legacy, which was heartening.

"I can teach Latin America," I told the department chair. "It was my second field." Perhaps it was the confidence that the U. of C. instilled, making us believe we could teach anything. Or perhaps it was my call to duty. The students needed the course. As homogeneous as the student population was, Valparaiso had nobly infused multiculturalism into the general education curriculum, requiring all students to take courses such as Latin American history.

"They do need this class," he replied. "And I have heard good things about you from your students." Knowing that made all the difference. Not just in that moment, but in the long trek ahead of forging a career path. I wanted so much to be good at teaching.

The students enrolled in my classes there differed significantly from my students at the other institutions – regional campuses of Purdue and Indiana University, which were both public schools. At Valparaiso they were more prepared for university study, more likely born of parents who had attended college, and had met admissions requirements that did not exist at the other campuses. Also, they were about 99.9% white, or at least it seemed so. That somehow made a difference. It does matter when teaching about the world. World history in itself is diverse, if written and told authentically. It is the history of all people. Among a more diverse student body I had been able to bring all their backgrounds into the human story, or I at least tried to. In this case, they would act more as observers, looking in from the outside. But so would I. I was white, too.

While we are physically detached from history, and when approaching it as an academic subject should remain intellectually so, there is a somewhat more disturbing disconnect when lecturing about the human story in a room full of white people. Teaching about the American Revolution, at least from a political and military perspective, was different. The majority of players in that story were white. Teaching about Latin America would pose new challenges.

"You're not Mexican," a student once told me years later on the first day of my first History of Mexico class.

"You're right. I'm not." It was a learning moment for me, as I discovered just how bold and provocative a student could be. It was a teaching moment, as well. "I'm not French either, but I can teach the French Revolution. Anyway, there is no one Mexican history. You will learn in this class just how culturally, socially, politically, and economically varied Mexico is, and how its history is packed with vastly different perspectives." I am not sure whether my reply satisfied him, but it served as a starting point for discussions through the semester on how history is written.

The Valparaiso class was not nearly as diverse, and I wondered how I might get them to feel connected to Latin

America. I casually made a comment about there being a major city in South America named Valparaiso, to see what their reaction might be. A prepared and studious group, some nodded while others wrote down what I said. Clearly they were serious, and it seemed they might take well to the semester curriculum I had planned for them. It would be challenging for them and me, as we covered at least a dozen countries from the time of their independence in the early 19th century to the present. The task of approaching history both chronologically and regionally presents unique demands when the subject is Latin America. It is far more complex than many realize. But that is one of the aspects I most wanted to emphasize, and I found myself adding to the complexity by giving substantial attention to the Caribbean. And if I were to do that, I could not ignore Haiti.

There were good reasons for including Haiti in the course design. First, it was part of Latin America. While other scholars might not consider it representative of the area, I knew if it were not included there it might not be covered at all. Second, Haiti was in the news. That is not always a good reason, as historians shy away from "presentism" – the examination of history through prisms of the present. However, I did not intend to encourage students to judge past actions in or regarding Haiti through late 20th century sets of cultural or moral criteria, which is what presentists tend to do. Rather, I wanted to make the material relevant for them. The Clinton Administration had recently intervened to give President Jean Bertrand Aristide his rightful place in power, and this might be a chance for my students to make better sense of Haiti's unstable past and understand why this move was so significant.

I also saw this as an opportunity to appeal to their religious sensibilities. While not every student professed adherence to a faith, Valparaiso is a Lutheran school, and religion permeates the campus environment. I assigned Aristide's recently released autobiography. It was not a typical choice for a history class, but it would prompt discussion about objectivity and how it is we come to know what we know. It would also add to the complex dimension of combining religion with politics so prevalent in Latin American history. In the work he discusses his past as a priest and his commitment to the poor. And he opens the door for real world applications of liberation theology.

Liberation theology is a delicate blend of New Testament Christian principles, particularly those of progressive Catholics, with the basic tenets of Marxism. Introducing the concept to students was new to me. In fact, the topic itself was fairly new to me. While considered controversial and in some circles dangerous, history professors discuss religion and politics all the time. Liberation theology was reasonably fresh, however, articulated only since the 1970s, and comparatively radical. Still it weighed heavily in the contemporary history of Central America and some parts of South America. Here was a chance to see how it played out, or was rejected, in the Caribbean. And it was a chance for me to learn more about it and learn more about Aristide.

While covering nearly two centuries of development of the majority of the Western Hemisphere, there was little time to devote to the subject. As an educator, I wondered whether merely scratching the surface of such a deep issue was worse than ignoring it altogether. But I am not sorry for introducing it. It helped them to jar their minds and imagine alternative belief systems, which is necessary in understanding the human story. And it helped me to learn more about Haiti, without knowing that this was just the beginning of a long journey.

3
HEARING ARISTIDE

My fascination with Aristide continued. Who was this man who so eloquently articulated the struggles of the poor, yet gained the support of the U.S. government? Backers of U.S. intervention under President Clinton argued that it was necessary in order to protect democracy and the electoral process there, but throughout the 20th century the U.S. had intervened repeatedly in Central America and the Caribbean to protect its own interests. Could this soft-spoken former priest survive as the first democratically elected President in Haiti after nearly two centuries of independence? The questions continued, and I cannot say I was ever truly satisfied in finding answers. Haiti was not my field of expertise and I never set out to investigate the truth of events there fully.

The U.S. did succeed in repositioning Aristide, and after serving out his term he stepped down. This was a clear sign that a clean, fair, sustainable electoral process might be taking root. It looked as if a peaceful exchange of power was possible. However, Aristide's prominence in political affairs did not come to an end. In a short time, there was talk that the might run for the office of President again. Still news regarding Haiti and discussions about Aristide subsided, and he seemed to be disappearing from the world scene. Then, in late 1999, I heard he was to make an appearance at a nearby conference on globalization. I had to attend.

My perception of Aristide changed, or perhaps deepened, when I had an opportunity to hear him speak. The conference was held at Governors State University, a small 4-year campus south of Chicago, and a seemingly unlikely place to host a former head of state. But the Haitian community in Chicago was strong, and with it, the support for Aristide intense. What he stood for was gaining more attention worldwide, as criticisms of neo-liberalism and the effects of globalization were permeating college campuses. A significant percentage of Governors State's students were minority, and their more progressive professors exposed them to stories of oppression and exploitation in the Caribbean and the rest of the world. The contemporary deepening of poverty in Latin America was seen as a result of neo-liberal policies orchestrated by the United States. Aristide remained a spokesman for the poor globally, and especially in Haiti. His message had been discredited by some, and those apparently threatened by his leadership engaged in character assassinations. At that point, however, I was there anticipating a visionary message grounded in peace. I arrived early as the auditorium began to fill not only with students, but also with faculty, staff, administrators, and many from beyond the campus community. The group included a significant number of Haitian-Americans from Chicago.

Aristide was a man small in stature and unobtrusive in demeanor, but he captivated his audience. Into his presentation it became clearer that he had a good number of vocal supporters in the auditorium. They shouted in agreement with what he was saying, and soon others began to protest in response. I had been in situations before where politics polarized a room.

But this felt more intense. There was something eerie about the atmosphere, and a bit confusing. I found the underlying tension discomforting, and concluded there was much more to the story of Aristide and Haitian presidential politics than I had understood.

There were calls from the crowd asking that he run again. He humbly replied that he had no plans to do so. A sense of friction grew and the pro- and anti-Aristide factions seemed more apparent. However, this was different from other events where ideological rivals debated, and political players were distanced from the seat of power. Even where events have erupted into shouting matches the arguments were grounded in differences of opinion – or subtle and not so subtle variations in ideology. While Aristide is considered by some simply an ideologue the conflict in that room felt based on something other than ideas. And I say felt, because I could feel it. Here there was a deeper sense of fear mongering permeating the space – because the stakes were higher, I thought. The poverty more profound, the road to development more difficult, the possibility for change more sharpened. I thought the thuggishness of the Duvalier era was gone, and here in suburban Chicago, what seemed thuggish tendencies remained. Had they taken their battle to Illinois? Was what Aristide stood for still considered that much of a threat?

Then the pro-Aristiders responded with equal intensity. In my mind there was no longer the meek, humble, peaceful, and poor on one side and the angry, threatening, and forceful on the other. The political behavior of Haitians seemed to be more complex than I had imagined. I thought about that complexity again years later, during a visit to Port-au-Prince in the fall of 2010. I sat in a restaurant following a wonderful early dinner of fish, rice, and rum punches. A friend of a friend had arranged for someone to keep me company while I waited for a ride to my hotel. I used my time alone to schedule a list of goals and office tasks for coming weeks in my planner; an activity more U.S. than Haitian. I would be returning to the States the following day, and as part of my cultural transition decided to embrace the idea of laying out what I wanted to accomplish in my research by week one, week two, and so on. It helped to pass the time, and somehow the work that lay ahead did not look so daunting under the influence of rum punches.

The companions arrived, and proved to be delightful conversationalists. This was a post-earthquake visit for me, and it was good to engage in lively talk in the midst of where destruction had been so severe just months before. The young man and woman were very well educated, clearly from the upper class, and noticeably fair-skinned. We talked politics, religion, and economics in ways deemed taboo in the States, at least with strangers. I mostly listened, trying to make better sense of things. I suppose we have a tendency to filter new information and experiences through a lens of familiarity. Race and class play such prominent roles in Latin American society that I could not help but allow my perceptions to be shaped by what I had already come to know through study and travel. I found myself sorting, classifying, and categorizing what was coming out of their mouths based on who I thought they were, or what group I thought they represented. Becoming conscious of this bothered me, as I had apparently evolved, or devolved, into someone who could not simply enjoy an exchange in that place and in that moment.

The young man – tall, lean, and strikingly handsome – had spent much time in the U.S. When the topic of Aristide arose, he was quite critical, and I attributed that to his race, class, and U.S. experiences. Without saying so openly – even after rum punches – I probed a bit deeper. He and the woman both agreed that they had held hope for Aristide and his promises early on, but became disenchanted. By this time, he had come to and left the presidency once more, and their youth suggested they had supported him in his more recent election. But they hinted at the use of intimidation against political enemies by those in his inner circle. Their tone and body language indicated they wanted to say more, but hesitated. I did not ask any more questions. Perhaps I wanted to keep a more idealistic version of Aristide in my mind.

4
CARIBBEAN IN
THE CLASSROOM

The semester I heard Aristide speak also marked the first time I taught a course devoted entirely to the history of the Caribbean. I was teaching full time at Purdue Calumet, though not yet on the tenure track. I had pressed to teach Latin American history there, in addition to U.S. History surveys and Women in America, letting my department chair know that things had gone well at Valparaiso. Normally a department would make a decision to create a position for a specialist in the area, but I did not foresee that happening. The curriculum at that time centered on the United States and Western Europe, and though courses in Latin America were still on the books, they had not been taught in years.

At first I was told they would not be popular, but I pointed out that my classes always filled. Plus, I was working for peanuts and was nothing if not cost-effective. I wondered what popularity had to do with the teaching of history anyway. Devoting a course entirely to the Caribbean was admittedly taking a chance and it would be a rare addition to history curricula in many parts of the country. But I believed the course was warranted. I had attempted to cover as much of the region as possible in my Latin American history surveys, but there just was not ample time to give it the attention I believed it deserved. The Caribbean has a unique and complex history which is not always easy to integrate with those of surrounding regions. Its inclusion in Latin American history at all is not common, at least regarding anything that occurred after the voyages of Columbus. And then, emphasis is given to the Spanish-speaking islands, or the Greater Antilles, or simply Cuba. By designating a separate course, I could devote more balanced attention to the French, English, and Dutch Islands, and examine the distinct – while sometimes combative – histories they experienced.

The response among students was great, but that from faculty colleagues not so much. Some looked down their noses, as Ph.D.'s often do. I was trying to become accustomed to that. What made things worse was that our academic advisor, a faculty member of equal rank who frequently defended the notion of American exceptionalism, joked with students about how my class would be meeting out on the lawn where we would all smoke *ganja*. Under other circumstances I might not have felt so threatened, but trivializing one's work in the academic arena can be tenure track homicide. What bothered me in addition were comments later made by a junior faculty member whose opinions I had come to respect. He was an up-and-coming scholar in the area of Atlantic history and his research was impeccable. I considered him a friend and valuable addition to the department. One night in a bar, where some of us gathered on Fridays, he asked about my work.

"I heard you teach the history of the Caribbean."

"Yes," I replied, eager for an intelligent exchange on our specialties.

"But nothing happened there," he said. "The Europeans discovered it, and the islands became nothing more than sugar producers for the empires." He basically suggested I was wasting a semester of my students' valuable time.

Instead of taking a moment to describe what it was that I taught, the books I used, or the methodology, I backed off. I had already spent too much time and energy justifying the inclusion of Latin America in the curriculum. The Latino student population of our campus was the largest of any in the state, and to deny them the opportunity to learn their history was, in my opinion, criminal. But I was not teaching it only for them. To omit an entire region from the curriculum was making a statement to all students that its contributions to the human story were insignificant.

I had grown sensitive to the tensions between Latino and black students and did not want to be too public in my pleas, for African history was also absent from our offerings. I was in no position to introduce courses on African history, but I hoped my growing passion for the Caribbean might influence the development of an effective class that included a substantive address of the African diaspora. And the cultural richness and diversity of the Caribbean might aid in breaking down any barriers that existed between black and Latino students. The lines become blurred in studying the Caribbean. In my world history survey classes I found myself zeroing in on the Caribbean as a microcosm of the world, where all of the major European empires vied with one another in colonization and battles for gold, silver, and gemstones through mining and piracy. Native populations quickly disappeared and were replaced by shiploads of Africans destined for harsh lives, and often early deaths, under slavery. Mulatto populations emerged where Europeans had sexual intercourse with Africans – often by force. Each island gave birth to a culture distinctly "New World" but with varying degrees of European influence, the most apparent of which was found in languages.

In one world history class I used Sammy Sosa as an example. Continually grasping for pop culture references to illustrate historical development and make it seem relevant, baseball came to mind. No one at that time could deny the exceptional promise of the Chicago Cubs. Not much of a sports fan, even I knew they were all the rage.

"So why might someone who looks like Sammy Sosa speak Spanish?" I asked one of my classes. "Where is he from?"

"The Dominican Republic?" one ventured to guess.

"Were a lot of slaves brought there, too?" another asked.

"Sammy Sosa is black?" I heard from a black student. She struck me from early on in the semester as someone who had never paid much attention to history before, but had reached an age when she became insatiably curious. She asked a lot of questions, and this one prompted a discussion regarding shades of skin color. She looked at her arm and agreed that she and Sosa were about the same shade. "I thought he was just very dark Spanish." I was not sure what that meant, but I took it as an indication that my instincts were right about the value of teaching Caribbean history.

While I could not expect complete acceptance from my department colleagues, a sense of camaraderie emerged unexpectedly at a subsequent conference of Latin Americanists. Meeting periodically with our counterparts at regional, national, or international conferences can satisfy us with the validation we need to be more effective on our own campuses. This is where we share ideas, present our research, obtain constructive feedback, learn what is new in our fields, and even share classroom tips. Conference attendance can give us the rejuvenation we need – a dose of oxygen, so to speak – and even an enlightening conversation over cocktails now and then, in a magnificent location if the organizers are lucky.

That was not the case with this one, scheduled on a dreary winter weekend in the rural Upper Midwest. Still, it is where I heard a most inspiring presentation on why the Haitian Revolution should serve as a key component of any Latin American History survey, and play an integral part in teaching about the Revolutionary movements that swept North America and Europe. This perspective had not yet been put forward in a way that reached many educators in the field. It was still the late 1990s, and Latin America as a whole had been given little attention within the wider context of world history. And among courses devoted to Latin America Haiti was often still missing.

The professor making the case was a reserved woman from the Dominican Republic, who taught at the University of Wisconsin-Stevens Point. Though I had long been enamored of the Wisconsin system, what I knew of Stevens Point was that it lay about three quarters of the way to our Upper Peninsula fishing destination where my family went each summer.

"Yes," I would tell my friends incapable of picturing me sitting in a boat on a lake, reeling in bluegill, "we drive through Wisconsin to get to Michigan." Stopping in Stevens Point for some locally brewed Point beer had become a ritual marking the true beginning of vacation. By that place in the trip the air had become more crisp and the evergreen trees more abundant. I wondered what the life's journey of a woman making her way from the Dominican Republic to northern Wisconsin must have looked like. My wonder did not distract me from what she was saying, however. Her case was strong.

She argued that learning about the Haitian Revolution was vital to understanding the Revolutionary Era as a whole. It lay at the crux of the period, between U.S. independence and the sweeping independence of Latin American nations reaching from Mexico – which then included the territory from California to Texas – all the way south to Chile and Argentina. As a French colony, the struggles in St. Domingue represented the dominant elements of the American Revolution, and then some. Demands for legislative representation within the empire, and then separation and the forging of an autonomous Haitian republic, reflected parallel events rooted in Enlightenment philosophy. But the movement also included widespread slave rebellion. Napoleon Bonaparte considered the colony's sugar profits so valuable to France that he was willing to sell Louisiana to the new United States in order to focus on keeping it within his empire. Once independent, Haiti was widely viewed as a black republic with no legitimate future, and the slave-holding U.S. President Thomas Jefferson refused to recognize it as a new nation.

I was deeply indebted to this professor for her work on the subject and the time she took to present it. If I am not mistaken, her paper was subsequently published in *The History Teacher*, a journal issued by the Society for History Education, an affiliate of the American Historical Association. My personal thanks to her at the time could not have been enough. Her perspective was not entirely new to me; rather, it reinforced and enhanced what I had already suspected. I found comfort in her work, knowing that I was not alone in my desires to see Haiti given its rightful place.

5
VOODOO

About halfway through my first semester teaching
Caribbean history, I thought it would be interesting to invite
a colleague to speak to the students about voodoo. We were
fortunate to have a Haitian-born adjunct faculty member
teaching in the Department of Foreign Languages, and she and
I had chatted here and there about Haitian history. She taught
Spanish, was fluent in French and Creole, and her primary
interest was literature. I was fascinated by her command
of languages and ability to integrate linguistics and culture
into her courses and conversations. My research in Cuban
Santería had ignited a special interest in syncretic religions,
and I wanted to learn more about what the parallels between
Santería and voodoo might be. Santería is considered by
some more genuinely syncretic – a clearer blending of Roman
Catholicism and West African Yoruban beliefs and practices,
while voodoo is primarily African.

Some Roman Catholics and Yorubans would disagree,
each either drawing Santería closer to their teachings, or
pushing it further away. Rituals, altars, offerings, and saints
representing various aspects of the world and answering
human prayers are present in each. To the academic observer,
comparable elements are apparent. In voodoo there are similar

parallels; however, many, especially Catholics, argue that there is nothing Catholic about it. Historically, Protestant colonists in the islands, particularly fundamentalists and Calvinists, viewed Catholicism and voodoo as equally wicked, and Catholics no less pagan than non-converted Africans. To them, Catholicism reeked of idolatry and had strayed from Christianity in its purist form.

Eternally fascinated by the many ways in which religion has influenced the human story, I had dabbled in historical explorations of these concepts. However, I was also aware that the theological rifts were not limited to the past. They lingered and I needed to keep that in mind when lecturing on religion in class. Some might advise avoiding discussions of religion altogether, but it is both absurd and unwise to ignore religion when teaching history. Academic approaches to religion are indeed possible, and I learned that as a college student myself. I attended a small Catholic school in Indiana, where we were required to take two courses in theology. I chose Introduction to Theology taught by a priest who assigned Huston Smith's *Religions of Man* as our main text. He also incorporated ongoing scientific discoveries regarding the universe that challenged man's contemporary understanding of life's origins. My education, worldview, and subsequent life were changed deeply as a result. The other class I chose, also taught by a priest, was The Old Testament. We learned when the Old Testament was written, how it was written, and why it was written. We learned about time and place and human players, as well as the politics of translation. We studied it as a historical document.

Those experiences helped empower me to be conscious and fearless when teaching. No subject is taboo when approached openly, honestly, and without bias. An on-again off-again Catholic, I was careful not to bring in my own opinions about the Church. The denominations of my students reached across the spectrum, and some declared themselves atheists. The vast majority had not taken a careful look at the origins of their own faiths, not to mention those of others. And I hoped to give them permission to learn more about all of them, even those they did not yet know – all without passing judgment. Then an incident arose in which I found myself passing judgment.

A history major who I had known from other classes enrolled in my Caribbean class. He had frequently taken advantage of office hours to engage me in numerous discussions of history, most of them not so deep, but some quite interesting. Then one day he made some disturbing comments about the enslavement of Africans. His exact words escape me, but he was essentially repeating some bizarre justification for slavery. I let him go on just a bit; not enough to let him believe I agreed with him, just enough to try to understand what he was thinking and how he came to think that way. His position did not make much sense to me, but he seemed to hold it with such certainty. His assertions included significant historical detail; false, but detail nonetheless. It was impossible for me to imagine he had learned anything like that in classes offered by my colleagues or in high school, so I asked him how he knew so much about the topic.

"My pastor is a fountain of history," he told me. "His sermons are so educational and I've learned so much from him." Oh my, I thought. "And what he says is not at all like what I have learned in school."

Thank goodness, I murmured under my breath. I asked him where he attended services. The church he described was one I had driven past many times. It was on the north end of the town where I lived, situated next to a park with basketball and tennis courts, soccer fields, and a picnic shelter, and surrounded by well-kept, middle class homes built in the 1970s and 80s.

I thought I knew the churches in town well. But at that moment, I realized that I understood nothing about this one except its location, appearance, and the word "Christian" in its name. It did not much matter to me where people went to church, but I am pretty sure I had not known anyone who was a member there. Mine was a medium-sized suburban town with at least one church or synagogue representing each of the following: Roman Catholic, Lutheran, Presbyterian, Methodist, Episcopalian, Byzantine Catholic, Christian Reformed, and Reform Jewish. There was also a smattering of smaller churches, and the megachurch on the sprawling south end of town with the Starbucks and life-sized mannequinesque representation of the Last Supper. Regardless of one's denomination there seemed to be a relatively open door policy and activities galore at many of them. Free gym time, blood drives, pancake breakfasts, and so on were held in adjoining rooms at various places of worship. For most of us, the only noticeable differences seemed to lie between those who sponsored bingo and church festival beer tents, and those who did not. Other than that, the whole religion thing seemed sort of average, and a sense of community trumped divisiveness.

But to learn there was pseudo-historian preaching in town disturbed me. I found it puzzling and, then again, disturbing. The student was a nice enough young man – enthusiastic, energetic, and dedicated. He was just being sold a bill of goods on the slavery thing. When I first heard Pat Robertson blame Haitians' centuries-long struggle with impoverishment on a pact with the Devil, I thought of this student. I pictured him listening intently to the preacher, just as he listened to me, somehow reconciling what I taught with a misguided take on history he believed was backed up by biblical teachings. We should be free to discuss all claims about history: that it is based on lies, that it is a fabrication intended to mislead, that it is purely literature, that man has taken no major step without the intervention of God, or that it is only the result of human will and we are indeed making progress. But those discussions should be grounded in intellectualism and critical thinking. No one of those interpretations should be presented as absolute truth. To say to even one of my students, from the pulpit, that the Atlantic slave trade was God's will, would make my job infinitely more difficult. But what concerned me most was a specific request made by this student.

The request came at a time of mounting culture wars, in which spewing venom claimed that U.S. universities were nothing more than liberal dens of iniquity and therefore dangerous to society. Perhaps I was becoming as suspicious of some preachers as they were of professors, and more than once I considered sitting in on one of their sermons to hear just what it was they were saying.

My gut whispered "beware" when the student asked if he could record the lecture on voodoo. I looked at the video camera in his hand. Class was just beginning and I had taken a seat near him, waiting for the presentation to start. This was before Youtube and Facebook had permeated our lives, but I knew the recording would likely be disseminated well beyond my classroom. I wondered what his intentions were. Students had occasionally made audio recordings of my lectures to aid them in studying for exams. But something about this request made me feel uneasy. I told him politely that we had not cleared a recording with the speaker in advance, so it would be inappropriate.

"I think she's ready to start," I told him, nodding as a signal for her to go ahead. He seemed frustrated but agreed, and set the camera next to his notebook. He gazed curiously and took copious notes, and it looked as if the camera may have remained on, capturing audio. I said nothing, believing that protesting too much might fuel a fear that something sinister was taking place.

The presentation was captivating, and what she said about voodoo was powerful. The students' eyes were transfixed on her, as were mine. She spoke of rituals, belief systems, and zombies. It complemented lectures from previous weeks, so students were as prepared as possible. I wondered how inviting her could have been interpreted as anything other than purely educational, and why he would want to search for something evil in the classroom experience. He seemed to like the courses I taught, and the way I taught them.

In retrospect, it seems this had nothing to do with me, and everything to do with voodoo. He may have simply seen this as a rare opportunity to gain an insight into Haitian culture and religion and preserve it; perhaps share it with people from his church, perhaps not share it with anyone at all. Any uneasiness was likely influenced by my own insecurity, as the teaching of Caribbean history continued to raise eyebrows among colleagues. It was worsened by the climate of fear-mongering and attacks on "liberal" universities. The subject never came up again, but an unnecessary wedge had been driven between teacher and student.

As the class ended that day, I thanked our speaker and then continued in conversation with her as the students left.

"That was wonderful," I told her. "Thank you for taking the time to share what you know."

"It was my pleasure," she replied. "It is good to learn

there is interest in my country."

"I would really like to hear more about your understanding of voodoo's impact on Haitian society. Maybe we could have lunch one day."

"That would be nice," she said. "There is much more to talk about." I truly looked forward to lunch with her, knowing full well how often faculty lunch plans fail to materialize. "I know someone who was put into an institution because of his zombie experience," she added.

"Really?" The idea of someone being treated for zombie delusions was fascinating, and the fact that she knew such a person made it even more so. "So are there doctors who specialize in dealing with people who think they are zombies?" I asked.

"No, he was a zombie." She spoke so matter-of-factly.

"What do you mean, he was a zombie?"

"We have a lot to talk about."

We never got around to having lunch. How in the world did I let that opportunity slip away? I agreed to find time in my schedule to proofread an article she had written, and did give her feedback. But we never made time to talk more about zombies. As happens with so many adjunct faculty, she was gone the following semester and I have no idea where she went.

6
CHANCE MEETING

My passion for researching and teaching Caribbean history continued to grow. I experimented with new reading assignments and devoted more resources to travel. Three visits to Cuba in three years, with stops in the Bahamas and Mexico's Yucatán Peninsula, helped to deepen my understanding of culture, politics, and economics. My continued education pulled me in unforeseen directions, and I felt increasingly detached from my friends and colleagues. Some were curious and supportive, but my experiences were taking me to places – both physical and intellectual – that I found difficult to describe. At the same time, work and social obligations served to keep me grounded in my other world. More and more, I felt as if I were living in two realities.

When the local chapter of the American Association of University Women asked if I would speak on "Women in the New Millennium" at its upcoming annual meeting, I could not think of anything I would like to do less. First, I was a historian. I looked back, not forward, so how could I possibly speak to that topic? Was is not a bit broad? And frankly, at that time I could not think of a more stuffy and dull audience. But I said yes.

When I arrived, I realized I was right. Those in the room did look stuffy and dull. I had given a similar speech in previous months, which is probably another reason why I was not looking forward to this. That presentation, for a group of businesswomen, was an unexpected hit. The event was a networking one held in a warm and cozy art gallery and the experience changed my opinion of women in business. I am a bit ashamed to admit they were far more energetic, engaged, and creative than I imagined they could be. And so welcoming. I wondered whether I had made a mistake in choosing a career in academia, where people could be so arrogant, judgmental, and depressing.

I clearly erred in repackaging my presentation for this group, or at least in hoping for an enthusiastic response. The room was large and formal, non-descript in its décor, and attendees sat motionless at round tables of ten or so. It was dreadful. I should have felt more at home than I did. After all, they were university women and I was a university woman. But I was feeling more and more alienated from all things university-related. On top of that, I was in the midst of acknowledging that my marriage was coming to an end. I did not want to be there. The thought of standing before a crowd extolling the accomplishments and potential of women made me sick to my stomach. Between greetings, I stared out the window. It was a warm spring afternoon and I knew my kids were at the ball park with their father. If there were anywhere at all I would rather be it was at the park.

The only saving grace was meeting a delightful woman at my table. Never particularly good at small talk, I was grateful to be seated next to someone so genuinely charming. Her smile and interest in things that mattered kept me going. The meal was fine, but I was not very hungry. After my presentation, I was just glad to sit down.

"So, you've really been to Cuba?" she asked.

"Pardon me?"

"You mentioned that you had traveled to Cuba. That must have been exciting." The talk had been a sort of out-of-body experience. It was a blur, and I couldn't remember exactly what I had said.

"Yes. Yes, it was. I learned a lot. It is a fascinating place."

"By any chance have you been to Haiti?" My ears perked up.

"Haiti? No, why?"

"It's next to Cuba. Just wondered." I was impressed she knew it was located near Cuba.

"Yes, it is. I remember being in Baracoa, in eastern Cuba, when our guide pointed to some heavy clouds and told us it must be raining in Haiti. That's as close as I've been. I'd love to go."

"There is a group planning a trip. If you're interested, I could give you their information."

"Well…" Any other time I would have said yes without hesitation. But I wondered how I could possibly do it now, knowing my family was falling apart. "I have been wanting to for such a long time."

"The organization is called the Heartland Center."

"Thank you," I replied. The Heartland Center. I wondered what kind of group this was, but it didn't really matter to me. I called the office later that afternoon expecting there might be a trip planned some distance in the future.

It turned out to be a Catholic group affiliated with the Diocese of Gary, which devoted its work to social justice issues both locally and globally. Its director, Father Tom Gannon, answered the phone himself. The exchange was eerily easy, and I felt as if I could talk with him for hours. The chance meeting with that anonymous woman would change everything, as it marked the beginning of a new path of discovery.

My marriage did end. I found it strange that a professor of mine had warned me years before when I entered graduate school that women who pursue advanced degrees often divorce. I denied anything like that would happen to me. To say that higher education causes divorce is reminiscent of 19th century claims that the rigors of graduate school pursuits caused sterility. "Experts" based their conclusions on the fact that highly educated women tended to have fewer children. There was no logical connection. And I could not imagine holding myself back on the chance it might preserve my marriage. But, for many reasons, we did grow apart. I was very much in love with him when we married, but nineteen years and three children later, we had little to say to one another. Following an argument one evening I asked him to leave, and he was gone by morning. I filed for divorce later that week.

We attempted briefly, and perhaps half-heartedly, to reconcile. It did not work. Living together again, we went on a Saturday night movie date as we had often done the past and were silent the entire ride home. In the driveway, in the dark car, we agreed to go through with the divorce. We promised to sit down together with the kids and break the news, doing our best to let them know everything would be all right. That was September 8th of 2001. I slept on the sofa.

On Tuesday, September 11, I sent the two older ones off to school. Katie was a junior and Danny was in seventh grade. Sam, then 9-years-old, and I engaged in our daily ritual of eating cereal and watching cartoons until it was time for him to leave. I kissed him good-bye, and told him again not to worry. He had always been more sensitive than the others, at least in ways more apparent. I sat down again on my newfound bed with my bowl of cereal, dreading going in to teach later in the day. I stared blankly at the television set.

When I realized I could be watching something other than cartoons, I changed the channel only to see smoke billowing from the first of the World Trade Center towers to be hit. I don't remember much of the rest of that day, except wondering whether I should somehow let my children know that I was aware of what was happening, and that I would be home from work as quickly as possible after they returned from school. I did not fear for their physical safety; rather, I just wanted to tell them again that everything would be all right. But I knew that it wouldn't. Not because of the terrorists, but because of me. I was taking away their innocence and feelings of security, and no one should ever do that to a child.

Visiting Haiti would have to be put aside temporarily, but I knew when the time was right, I would go. That time came a couple years later.

7
HEARTLAND CENTER

I looked forward to the preparatory meetings with members of the Heartland Center and others participating in the trip. They were held in a former classroom of a local Catholic school, no longer used due to declining enrollment. Father Gannon – or Tom, as we came to call him – was as interesting as my mother advised he would be.

"You'll like him. He's a Jesuit," she told me. She had heard his sermons while he performed monthly Mass duties in town.

"Why?" I asked her. I wondered what she knew of Jesuits' work. It was not the kind of thing we discussed. She was a dutiful Catholic, but it never occurred to me she differentiated Jesuits from the other religious orders. My grandmother's brother was a Jesuit who taught at the University of Detroit, but we just knew him as Uncle Pete, the priest. Perhaps my mother knew more about theology and the reputation of his order than I realized.

"He knows so much, and he speaks in outline form. Something a professor would like."

She was right. The first time I heard him give a sermon he quickly stood out among the other priests I had heard. If I had not known he was a Jesuit, I might have figured it out.

Perhaps it was his sense of logic and wealth of knowledge, but more likely it was his bold stance on justice. It is not that priests of other orders are not committed to social justice, but there is just something about the Jesuit way.

In preparing for the Haiti trip, he immediately earned my trust. This was not what could be considered a typical mission trip. I did not want to dismiss the work of others nor did he, but this project was not designed as charity or a short-term feel good experience for those who opted to go. To be honest, I would have gone anyway. But this made me more comfortable. We held serious discussions about the differences between charity and justice, how achieving justice was more challenging and perhaps apt to upset the social and economic position of those accustomed to giving a helping hand to those in need. True justice might exist only in a system where the poor were not kept poor and dependent upon the charity of others. He was not as radical in his activism as he might have been, but intellectually he understood the distinctions and conveyed his positions eloquently.

We did not dwell on ideas too much, as we had practical matters to deal with – itineraries, flight arrangements, malaria preventatives, and so on. A representative from Catholic Relief Services helped us with the details. The organization was extraordinarily active on the ground and considered one of the most successful in making things happen in Haiti. She would make arrangements to meet us there.

Our group would include Tom, Fran, who worked in the Heartland Center office, and Bishop Dale Melczek. There would also be Carol, a woman actively engaged in her parish and committed to all kinds of justice issues; Louise, equally active in her parish and fearlessly devoted to such practices as teaching reading to inmates at the local state prison; and

Monica, incredibly compassionate and insatiably curious about the world's religions and spiritual teachings. John, a young photographer from the local paper also accompanied us. I felt a like an outsider, as I had strayed quite a bit from the Catholic faith over the years, and in my mind referred to the other women as the "church ladies." But I could not imagine a more interesting and wonderful group of traveling companions.

We would be serving as a delegation from the diocese, there to learn and then report our observations to parishioners back home. Tied to the project were fundraising efforts, primarily the planning of special collections taken during the Mass. We each paid for our own expenses, so any money raised would go directly to the project. Fundraising was not one of my strengths, but the more I learned of the work in Haiti, the easier it became.

The venture resulted from a recent initiative begun by the U.S. Conference of Catholic Bishops. Its purpose was global solidarity, and through its implementation they hoped to see their dioceses partner with people-driven projects in various parts of the world designed with long-term development in mind. From what I understood, Bishop Melczek had been actively committed to the idea at the national meeting and enthusiastically brought word of it back to Gary. After much deliberation with Tom and others, a partnership was forged in Haiti. The poverty was severe and the country was geographically close, contributing to the sad irony of economic disparity in North America and also facilitating travel there.

While Catholic Relief Services representatives described a variety of undertakings in need of assistance, they decided on one devoted to soil conservation in a remote area in northeast Haiti, near Fort Liberté. It involved the replanting of vegetation to ward off further erosion, a very serious problem in much of the country. In addition, it served to create a micro-economy in which participants could sell some of their produce in the marketplace. The notion of supporting Haitians in their own economic development appealed to me, as did agriculture. Haiti continued to rely on agriculture, and the benefits of producing from the earth while protecting it seemed boundless.

Tom recognized that soil conservation was unlikely to get parishioners' attention to the point of freely opening their wallets, but orphanages would. Orphanage work is tied to long-term development only tangentially, but there certainly was a need for financial assistance. They were non-existent in rural areas where we would spend much of our time, as people in small villages tended to look after one another, particularly children who had no means of support. But in Port-au-Prince orphanages were abundant. The need was great, not only for children whose parents had died, but also for those whose parents could not afford to provide for them. They were not always run well, and to some extent had become one of the few ways to make money from the outside. But we were assured some were very good, and we would visit a few in order to make a wise decision on where to channel some of the money collected back home.

This was one part of the trip that I did not look forward to at all. The thought of visiting orphanages frankly yanked at and twisted my gut. The only experience I had that came close was in junior high. One holiday season my Girl Scout troop visited the nearby Carmelite Home for Boys where we played games and made bell-shaped ornaments out of paper cups, pipe cleaners, glitter, and pictures cut from old Christmas cards. Such experiences can bring joy, I suppose, but this one brought me nothing but sadness. It shined a very bright light on how sheltered I had been, which perhaps was the intention of our troop leader. I did not understand how a day of game-playing and craft-making was of any help to the boys. After that I never looked at my own parents, or my situation as a loved and cared for daughter, the same as before.

Now that I was a parent myself, a visit to an orphanage seemed more heart-wrenching than I could imagine. My mothering instincts had kicked in, and at the same time I could not judge anyone who might have to turn over their children to someone else. Whatever the situation was, it could only be somehow attached to pain. I prayed the orphanage visits would take up only a small portion or our trip, and I kept my eyes on the soil project, the planet, and the potential for economic growth.

In retrospect my aversion for anything emotional was probably due to the fact that my own heart was so vulnerable at the time. In the two years since I first heard of the Haiti project, I spent much time ruminating about my failed marriage, yearned desperately to recreate a sense of security for my children, and had fallen in love with a man who moved across the country. The liaison was brief, confusing, and lacked any sense of closure. We had met as he was considering jobs far from Chicago, and I did not yet trust my judgment about men. It did not make sense to me that I felt such a deep connection with someone I barely knew, and I cared so much about him that I let him go without telling him how I felt. Neither the pain nor wonder went away. I just kept busy with other things.

8
Faith Remembered

Once I realized the Haiti trip was affiliated with the diocesan mission of peace and social justice, my fading connection with Catholicism seemed to strengthen. My relationship with the Church had been complicated. Many academics are detached from religion, but I never really was. Not totally. And any disconnection that did exist began long before.

During my teen years I had dreaded getting up early on Sunday to attend Mass with my family. I was the oldest of five; the youngest was my baby sister eleven years behind me. Mass-going was a ritual for my parents and they never missed. So we never missed. There was nothing in the teachings of the Church that I had any particular problems with at that time. In fact, much of it was meaningful to me. But I thought that some of the priests were out of touch, or just plain boring. There was some pretty good stuff in the Bible, even if I did not take it literally. But having a priest synthesize, analyze, and sermonize it for me seemed unnecessary when I wanted to think for myself. It was rare that they could provide any additional insight, at least for my teen mind.

One serious problem I had with going to Mass at that age stemmed from my expanding capacity for detecting hypocrisy. Coming of age in a Catholic setting was great for honing my "right-from-wrong" detectors. So when I saw people at weekly Mass who I had deemed as unscrupulous, I questioned why I should have to go. Looking back, I don't even remember who it was that I thought had done something unchurchly, or what gave me the idea I had anything to say about it.

"I don't know why I should have to go to Mass every Sunday," I told my mother. "There are hypocrites there."

"That's no excuse," my mother replied. "It doesn't matter what other people do with their lives. Anyway, that is not for you to decide. Just go to church." My mother was the least judgmental person I had ever known. And she was unwavering about Mass attendance.

I later got married outside the Church, by a judge, to a Jewish man. My parents loved him and even offered their backyard for the wedding. They were that non-judgmental. And they said nothing about my lack of Mass attendance after the wedding or about not raising my kids Catholic. But I began to miss the ritual and the sermons, the singing and the sacraments. I had left them behind only to avoid offending my husband and his family. I wished it weren't so, but often participating in anything Christian is construed as anti-Semitic. Rather than argue, I stayed away.

When my marriage ended, one of the first things I did was go to Sunday Mass at St. Thomas More, my childhood church. I felt afraid and lonely, and sought the security it had brought when I was young. I sat a few pews behind where my family used to sit. My mother and father arrived just after I did, reached their row, genuflected, and knelt down for a pre-Mass prayer. From that moment until the end of mass, I wept.

I understood that receiving Communion was out of the question. In grade school we were taught that people could not receive Communion with sin on their souls, removable only by the sacrament of Confession. Missing Mass was one of those sins, and I had missed for nearly two decades, except for an occasional holiday, wedding, or funeral. Considering my marriage to a Jew, I must have been judged guilty of fornication and a whole slew of other things. At the end of Mass, my parents saw me as they turned around to leave. I thought my mother would faint. She just looked to the floor and grinned. And that was that.

It was the social justice aspect of Catholicism that struck a chord in me. I had a big dose of it growing up in the 1960s. My studies in Latin American history put much of the Vatican II transformation into perspective, and I became enamored with Latin American Catholicism, particularly the grassroots kind. Speaking with leaders of the Haiti project, I was encouraged to become actively involved in the Commission for Peace and Social Justice at St. Thomas More and made plans to be present at the next meeting. During my long absence I had learned much about Thomas More, the man, and his teachings on social justice, bringing an added dimension to my new participation. This fresh relationship with the Church made things meaningful again and my newfound passion must have been apparent to the others at that first meeting.

It was early evening and getting dark as I entered the church office. The doorway to the meeting room was just a short way down the hall, and light poured onto shelves of books and a portrait of the Reverend Robert B. Weis. Father Weis founded the parish, and served as pastor for all the years I was growing up. I felt like I had come home again and if the Holy Spirit had ever been alive within me, it was then. I entered the room in the center of which was a long, heavy, wooden conference table, and introduced myself to the women who were there. I told them I would be reporting on the Heartland

Center's project in Haiti. It was one of those moments when one realizes that so many things experienced earlier in life had led to this point. I thanked God for being patient through my winding journey.

"Are you a member of the parish?" one of the women asked, peering over her glasses.

"Um…" She caught me off guard and I was not sure how to answer.

"I haven't seen you here before," another noted. I suddenly felt I was somewhere I shouldn't be. All of the depth and breadth of my understanding of the universal church and God and humanity and goodness and justice could not outweigh the gate-keeping nature of those women.

I made my presentation somewhere after a discussion of an upcoming blood drive. I was careful not to go too far in attempting to explain the need for economic and social restructuring in underdeveloped places like Haiti. Authentic social justice can indeed call for radical changes, but this was a time to keep things simple. I just told them the basics of the project, emphasizing the one of orphanage support and reminding them that the bishop was behind this. I figured if they were sticklers about my church membership status, they were likely followers of the bishop's authority.

Not long after that meeting I returned to the parish office to inquire about becoming a member. Maybe it was the eight years of Catholic school that urged me to play by the rules or a sense that if I had some official backing of the church office, no one could make me feel excluded. I had felt an allegiance to St. Thomas More parish and still had fond memories of school and my class marching down to Mass on Mondays, Wednesdays and Fridays. I did not want the fact that I had married a man I loved who happened to be Jewish to rob me of any possibility to preserve those memories with fondness.

The woman sitting behind the counter looked up when I came into the office.

"May I help you?" she asked.

"I would like to become a member of the parish," I told her. I was sure to say it as if I had just moved into town and had a perfectly normal and consistently Catholic history.

"Have you been attending Mass here?"

"Yes," I replied. "In fact, I went to school here and even remember the old church. Before they built this one, where we're standing, the area was all covered with grass and there were monkey bars over there and once I fell off and my mother had to pick me up from school and take me to the emergency room. My nose wasn't broken but there was blood all over the front of my white blouse…" I could not lie. And I could not seem to stop. The memories of being part of the parish all came flooding back. And I wanted so much to convince her that I deserved to be an official member.

"You'll have to fill this out." She handed me a two-sided form.

"You can take it home and bring it back later, if you like."

"Thank you," I replied. I walked out the door and stood on the step next to the stone statue of Jesus, looking out toward the area where we used to jump rope.

"Florida oranges tap me on the back, on the back, on the back…" I could almost make out young ghosts of my friends, their navy blue skirts flying and knee socks sliding down their calves. This time I felt as if I were almost there, just needing to fill out one sheet of paper, front and back. The sun glowed brightly over the parking lot once a playground.

I looked down at the form. "Name… Address…

Phone Number... etc., etc. Marital Status." Ouch. "Number of children... Date(s) of baptism." My heart sank. They had not been baptized. They were 9, 13 and 17 by then and trying to introduce the idea of baptism at that point would have created havoc in their lives.

I took the paper home and did not return it. I did return to Mass, however, but did not take Communion. I dutifully sat, letting people climb over me as they went up to the altar, and politely stood in the aisle as they returned to their pew, wondering what it was like and whether I would recognize the taste. I wished to be invisible, sitting in a pew toward the back, working on the Haiti project in my head, planning lessons about the history of poverty in Latin America, pretending to be Catholic, and wondering whether God cared one way or the other.

9
GETTING THERE

Gathering at O'Hare provided an opportunity for all of us to be together for the first time. Only Tom had been to Haiti, and perhaps the bishop. I had been to El Salvador a few years before and it was the only other time I had observed extraordinarily deep and rampant poverty that reached mile after mile after mile after mile. I anticipated something similar in Haiti. Because of Tom's experience, we followed his lead.

The first leg to Miami was similar to any such flight, with a mixture young and old traveling for business or pleasure. The trip from Miami to Port-au-Prince was very different. There were some Haitians, but the majority of passengers were clearly not. They mostly traveled in groups, as did we; and they were white, as were we. Each group took on its own personality. Ours was pretty eclectic and while fairly upbeat we tended to be a bit solemn. Perhaps it was due to the fact that we did not know each other well, but I attributed it to acknowledgment of what lay ahead. Others, however, seemed to be on some kind of high. A Jesus high. Many were wearing matching t-shirts, signifying they were with one another. The shirts generally noted a particular church and some message of hope and/or help. I did not really envy the giddiness that they exhibited; rather, I sat in wonder. We kidded with Tom, asking why we did not get matching t-shirts.

"We're already going to stand out there," he said, shaking his head. "We want to blend in with the community as much as possible, not set ourselves apart." That was not to judge others who go on group mission trips, but it is harder to feel a member of the family of man while wearing something that distinguishes you from others. I also wanted to be very careful not to judge their intentions. Before the trip some of my friends admonished me for wanting to go there to convert people. They were quite critical of conventional religion and assumed that was the point of my visit since I was traveling with the bishop, a priest, and some church ladies. I assured them that the idea of converting anyone to anything could not have been further from my mind. For me, this trip was just another step in my journey as a perpetual learner. I was going there as a student of the planet, a student of life.

When we arrived the air was warm and moist, a welcome change from January in the Midwest. Our spirits were light with the bustle of the airport and people were excited to meet us there. Moving quickly through a corridor I looked up and saw a sign that read "VIPs" above a doorway. I laughed, knowing just how gritty most of my travels had been. Jeans and backpacks normally served as the basis of my dress code, and I was more comfortable in a tent than a five-star hotel. Before I could comment, we were whisked through the doors. At that moment I realized this would not be like other trips. We were, after all, acting as a delegation and accompanying a bishop. Throughout our stay, he was humble and gracious, but there was a certain level of decorum expected. We were indeed treated as VIPs.

For our stay in Port-au-Prince Tom had chosen an older hotel that he referred to as one of faded elegance. He had traveled many of the world's major cities and was quite a connoisseur. He knew fine accommodations, fine food, and fine wine, but also knew this was not the time or place to be too extravagant. He did make us a promise, which he kept, of one lunch at the Hotel Oloffson so that we might experience the setting which spawned Graham Greene's *The Comedians*. For now we would settle in at a place just as welcoming but more simple. After a wonderful meal, we relaxed by the pool.

Having lived in the Midwest all my life, sitting by any outdoor pool in January was a treat. The bishop decided to take a swim. Avid about fitness, it was an opportunity he could not pass up. It was a bit unnerving at first, for the only time I had ever been in close proximity to a bishop was at my Confirmation. I was young and tried desperately to make sense of notions of grace, the Holy Spirit, and my new responsibilities as a soldier of Christ. I took Dorothy as my Confirmation name, and she was later erased from the books, no longer a saint, presumably because it was discovered she was not good enough. That chapter in my life made Catholicism very confusing to me. We learned to bow our heads and call the bishop "Your Excellency" making this event in which a subsequent bishop swam laps before me all the more strange.

At night the patio area was dimly lit, as is most of the world outside the United States. Electricity is just too precious. The painted wood façade of the hotel was decorated with carved trim, reminding me of something German or Swiss, or perhaps Victorian. I learned later that this architecture dots the cityscape of Port-au-Prince. After the others retreated to their rooms, I continued to talk with Tom. His experiences and take on life endlessly intrigued me, and I could have listened to him all night.

"My mother told me that I would like what you had to say," I said.

"Why?" I am sure he did not know how to respond.

"I think she was trying to get me to go to Mass again."

After a couple of rum punches I let him know it was Catholic social action, and in particular the trip planned for Haiti, that brought me back to the Church.

"After my divorce, it was comforting to come back, like seeing an old friend." He smiled. "Going to Mass reminded me of who I used to be." Before I knew it, I was confessing everything that the Church had meant to me, and that although I separated my faith from my lectures, teaching the history of Latin America had become a vocation of sorts.

On my third rum punch, the tears started flowing. I described my marriage and divorce, and how much I missed receiving Communion. He smiled and said that it would be all right, that the very idea of a "catholic" Church was one of openness and inclusion. I had gone to official Confession many times in my life, but had never felt more absolved of digressions than I had in that instant.

The next morning as the bishop said Mass at a small church nearby, I bravely walked up to receive Communion. He gave me an unsettling look as he held the host before my eyes. I had let him know in a casual introductory conversation at the airport that I had been divorced and was not much of a practicing Catholic. And it was true, I was not. Certainly not in comparison to the others in the group. He knew that I should not be receiving Communion and he knew that I knew. But that did not stop me.

"The body of Christ," he said carefully. He placed it in my hands.

"Amen." My response was barely audible. The host tasted just as I remembered. Only better.

10
OPPORTUNITY AND REGRET

The trip from Port-au-Prince to the soil conservation project required a short plane ride to Cap-Haïtien followed by a long drive. I looked forward to seeing just how small the plane was. And it was indeed small – just room for the eight of us, plus two guides, the pilot, and co-pilot. Boarding such a small craft brought to mind the wonder and delicate nature of flight, as we carefully situated ourselves and our belongings to balance the weight evenly. Once seated, I took a deep breath knowing there were plenty of prayers accompanying the group and any from me would not have added much. The sound of the engine made it difficult to chat, but the flight was good, as long as it lasted.

About 45 minutes into what was supposed to be an hour-long flight, the co-pilot turned to inform us that we would need to head back. After an exchange of words I could not decipher we learned that it was impossible to land due to fog. The single light at the Cap-Haïtien airport had burned out days before and had not yet been replaced. Evidently other flights had landed successfully, but it seemed the combination of thickening fog and the presence of the bishop made the pilots especially cautious.

We landed back at the regional airport in Port-au-

Prince and waited for a later flight. By this time we were very hungry (which becomes a relative term in Haiti) and a little wobbly from the early morning travels to nowhere, but we had bonded well and were becoming a chatty group. We did not mind sitting there and getting to know each other better while we waited indefinitely. And it gave us time to reflect on what we had already witnessed on the trip.

"Hey, Monica. Do you have anything to eat in there?" one of the others asked, pointing to her large tote. In our short time together, Monica earned the reputation of being the most thorough packer of the group. It is always good to have one, and it was especially fortunate for me, as she was my roommate.

"I'm sure she does," I replied.

"Yes, I do," she said. "What would you like?" She listed an array of healthy snacks so vast that even she found it amusing. We decided on Luna Bars. We also purchased some small, freshly-made meat pies from a woman working at the airport. I tried to imagine what she would think of the food courts at O'Hare. But nothing there could have been more satisfying than what she provided for us.

After two or three hours we boarded another plane, as the skies in Cap-Haïtien had reportedly cleared. By the time we landed and drove to our destination it was late afternoon. We were to meet with a group of community leaders to hear about the status of development projects in the area and were determined not to disappoint them. When we arrived, they were absolutely delighted. They had heard about our travel delays and assumed we would not come at all.

"Of course, we would be here," the bishop told them. We would not miss this opportunity." I could tell he meant it. Seated in a classroom-type space among a dozen or so Haitians working in education, agriculture, and health sectors, we watched and listened as Bishop Melczek and Father Tom spoke. But they more often listened. Yes, there was much work to be done, but people were doing it. It was very heartening. Following the exchange we had a chance to speak with one another. A man approached me and introduced himself.

"You are a teacher," he said. I looked at him, puzzled, and then realized we had each said a few words about ourselves to the group. He remembered.

"Yes, I am."

"I am a teacher, too." We had the most wonderful conversation. It turned out that he was an English teacher in the area. As we went on it became apparent that his English was not very good at all. Any Creole on my part was non-existent. I had studied only one year of French in high school and at that point the only thing I might have been able to verbalize was the first verse of *La Marseillaise*.

"I'm sorry," I told him, feeling as frustrated as he appeared.

"Do you speak Spanish?" he asked. His town was located very near the Dominican border and many Haitians in the area spoke Spanish.

"Yes, yes. My Spanish is much better than my French," I assured him.

"And my Spanish is better than my English," he said. So we proceeded in Spanish. It was one of the most memorable moments of my life. Still, when it comes to mind the memory is accompanied by a pang of guilt. In the conversation I promised to send him some books when I returned home. He was teaching English with no books, a common practice in Haiti, and he admitted he would use them himself to improve his own skills. I knew I would be able to gather some useful materials, including English-French, English-Spanish, and

French-Spanish dictionaries.

It is not at all easy to ship books to a place like Haiti and here we were, far, far from Port-au-Prince. But I was told that Catholic Relief Services would deliver them for me on a future trip if I could just send them to their Baltimore office.

I never did. Once adjusted to the way of life back home, with all the demands of work and the rest that daily routines take from a person, it is too easy for the experiences of such a remote place to slip away. There is no excuse, but it happens. As months passed, I wondered if Catholic Relief Services would even remember or be able to find him. Procrastination had paralyzed me in the past, but this time I felt as if I had broken a promise. Even now, nearly ten years later.

11
Soil

The ride up into the hills outside Fort Liberté made it apparent how Haiti earned its native name meaning "high land." The roads were steep and winding. It also became apparent what severe soil erosion looked like up close. Bare peaks, once covered with trees, were now home to thin, short grass barely strong enough to hold the earth in place, and where it was dislodged, huge pieces of hillside had fallen away. The extremities of drought and torrential rains were more than the hillsides could bear.

Trees had disappeared over the years, often used to make charcoal for cooking. Their removal made the land fragile and susceptible to erosion. In low-lying areas, goats devoured much of the remaining vegetation. Replacement through strategic planting had not been organized by the government in any systematic way, and it appeared on our visit that there were no such programs in sight. There had been a few smaller scale attempts by outsiders including ourselves at this point and they enjoyed varying degrees of success.

There are multiple advantages to strategic planting. First, adding roots, stems or trunks, and leaves at the soil's surface can significantly reduce the disappearance of earth, keeping the terrain intact. Second, given time, a future source of wood might be produced. This would require patience and long-term vision, but once established, cutting might be alternated with continual replanting introduced to maintain the supply. Third, the cultivation of vegetables and fruit producing trees could better feed the population. At the time of independence, Haiti had been the most agriculturally profitable of the island colonies, albeit with sugar. Clearly the land and climate made it possible to produce ample foodstuffs. And last, agricultural production might stimulate the economy by generating income, even on a small scale.

The project of the Gary Diocese was not the first attempt at soil conservation in the Department of the Nord-Est. Several years before, the United States Agency for International Development (USAID) had begun a planting program there. Well-intentioned perhaps, USAID was criticized for failed projects in Latin America and elsewhere. Policies and programs were developed in Washington, D.C. with little regard for ideas or input from the people of the underdeveloped world themselves. This was what happened in the Nord-Est. With funds from U.S. taxpayers, USAID officials decided which plant varieties would be grown and subsequently provided the seedlings to Haitians. But the plants were not cared for. Had the Haitians been included in the decision-making and planning processes in an authentic way, it is likely the project would have enjoyed greater success.

Learning from failed paternalistic undertakings, some non-governmental organizations (NGOs) working in the country have been careful to consider Haitians as equal partners or leaders in various projects. That was the case with this social conservation project, guided by the Global Solidarity Partnership. With funding from U.S. Catholics, the project was facilitated by Haitian agronomy experts educated in Port-au-Prince and formerly employed by the ministry of Agriculture. They held meetings with residents of the area who decided what they wanted to grow. Through micro-financing, they were able to purchase seeds, seedlings, fertilizer and farming equipment. Their grown vegetables would feed them and their families, and any surplus could be sold for profit, which would be used to repay the loans. From what we could see – and we were there only on a follow-up visit – after a couple years of operation things seemed to working well.

As soon as we saw it, we were impressed. After miles of slow and at times treacherous driving across a denuded landscape, the small farm emerged on the horizon, not unlike an oasis in the midst of a desert. It was green, beautifully varied, and carefully cultivated. The families that supported it, and in turn were supported by it, stood alongside their work with pride. Well organized plots of vegetable plants were thriving, due to produce a bountiful harvest in coming weeks. I could not help but notice the stark contrasts between Port-au-Prince and this place. It was quiet, calm, and spacious. The silence of the countryside is so deep, were it not for insects and other creatures one might even hear the vegetables grow. The differences were in many ways similar to those between Chicago and the rural Midwest that lay beyond its exurbs. The asphalt, concrete, and steel skyscrapers of urban centers feel noticeably detached from the natural earth from which they rise. In detachment from the land comes detachment from food. But here it was so close; within our reach. In this peaceful green valley there grew nutrition at their fingertips – fingertips that had been worked hard thus far and that would work hard again during harvest time.

Small houses had been constructed along the plantings' boundaries for the farmers and their families. One woman was gracious enough to welcome us into her home. This was one of the moments in which I imagined how different out visit might have been if not traveling with the bishop. She absolutely beamed as she guided us through the door. Many Americans let people into their homes only reluctantly, especially people they have never met. But that is not the case in Haiti, and it certainly was not the case with her. Perhaps she was happy to have any visitors at all in this hard-to-reach area, but she seemed particularly thrilled to play hostess to the bishop. She kindly led us to the living area where we sat on wooden ladder-back chairs. There seemed to be just two rooms and a dirt floor.

As I half listened to the conversation translated from Creole to English and then back again, I wondered how her family ate together and slept. She had eight children, she told us. I had heard of the high birth rate and realized I was seeing it firsthand. It seemed impossible that they could fit comfortably in this home. We were introduced to two of the older children, already in their late teens and more than six feet tall. Their labor was immeasurably valuable to the family enterprise, allowing them to produce more for market. But how did they sleep? For most of their lives, my children had their own rooms. This is admittedly a waste of space, considering the planet as a whole, but very common in the United States. Growing up I shared a room with two sisters, and then three when my baby sister came along, but our room was 15 feet by 15 feet, with an attached full bathroom. This house consisted of two rooms that could not have been more than 10 feet by 12 feet each. These living conditions illustrated what I had learned in earlier research and from previous drive-by visits to other underdeveloped regions, but this was the first time I sat in someone's own home for a heart-to-heart talk. It all became clearer. More real.

They had no electricity. I had lived without electricity due only to comparatively brief power outages caused by wind and ice storms, and for maybe three days while camping "to get away from it all." I even did it with kids. But I struggled to imagine doing it day in and day out and feeding eight growing children including teenage boys. It was dim inside on this overcast day and I imagined her working under the small window in the cooking area with few hours of daylight. Still, she could not have been more calm and pleased that we were there. We got up and said our goodbyes, and she continued to smile. As we drove away, I turned around and saw her sons going back to work. I remembered how I had found some of my own attempts at gardening just too difficult, and I was sorry for that. The vivid green surrounding her home became more distant. I turned back. Looking ahead, all I could see were bare hills.

12
ON THE GROUND

Somewhere along the road between the soil project and Fort Liberté we stopped at a women's artisan cooperative. It seemed to lie halfway between the middle of nowhere and the other side of eternity. We were tired from a long day of traveling, but eagerly got out of the trucks and stretched our legs. When we entered, it became clear that they had spent much time preparing for us. Several women sat neatly dressed, forming a large half circle against the wall and displaying the many colorful things they had made. Walking into their shop was like entering into a dimly lit wonderland. I speculated about where the women lived and how they got there. It had been such a difficult journey for us.

The long day of traveling in two separate Land Rovers had posed one muddy challenge after another. The landscape had consisted of endless fields dotted with goats and an occasional small block house. Where there were houses there were children, but they were few and far between. Shades of green against a gray sky swiftly growing darker had offered an eerie beauty. The road ahead, behind, and underneath was nothing but mud. The area had gone months with very little rainfall, but in the few days before had been deluged with several inches. Dirt had turned to thick muck and the roads were barely passable. When dry, the drive would have taken three and a half hours, but due to the poor conditions, it was taking six or seven. We lost track of the time and became a bit delirious. The drivers were incredibly adept at dodging ruts and holes and working diligently to avoid skidding off the road altogether. It was exhausting just to maintain a grip on the handle inside the vehicle to avoid hitting the ceiling and each other.

Hours into the ride, our driver stopped where a group of boys were playing. He spoke to one of them in Creole, and I wanted so much to know what they were saying. They seemed to be negotiating something. Then the older of the boys walked ahead, as we followed. The group waded slowly down, deeper and deeper, until the muddy water reached their waists. I turned around and looked out the back window to see that the other vehicle was close behind.

"I offered them a little, about a dollar, to see how deep the water is," the driver said. It seemed like a dangerous proposition to me, but the boys smiled and eagerly took on the task. We were careful not to give money to the children who begged at the airport, but this somehow seemed money well-spent and well-earned. The driver was Haitian, and we trusted him to do what was best. Eventually we came out on the other side without stalling the engine. The boys jumped and laughed, and took their pay. The depth and breadth of poverty and the dismal chances of finding ways to exchange money for goods and services was becoming more apparent.

After some miles of silence Fran and I joked and wondered aloud how the residents of the area might develop a market for mud. We considered the money spent on mud baths in the U.S. and thought about how we might draw well-to-do world travelers to rural Haiti for spa treatments. Time on the road permits wild unfolding of imagination and in no time I envisioned a Vegas-type opulent stone and glass resort with mud fountains pouring into pools lit ever so subtly and self-absorbed Americans sitting in them, up to their necks in brown goo. Haitian women would bring an endless supply of towels and men would bring and endless supply of rum punches. The perfect match of supply and demand, an intricately balanced economy. After some contemplation, I wondered whether it would differ much from the thousands of other lavish constructions situated among the poor in the "more successful" Caribbean islands.

Better yet, they might just bottle their mud for export without the risk of outsiders transplanting themselves in ways that might disrupt nature and the lives of locals. Yes. Just package millions of small portions of this endless supply in jars of 4.7 ounces or some such random amount. A special formula might be developed for soaking one's feet as an essential first step to one's pedicure. Just the right addition of natural ingredients could soften the cuticles and cracked heels, especially after too many days at the beach.

And there would be different scents – however that might be done – and then unscented for ever so sensitive and delicate white skin. And it would have anti-aging properties, of course, for who would buy anything these days that does not have anti-aging properties? And some doctor or other credentialed specialist would test it in an elaborate, well-equipped lab, to confirm its anti-aging properties for just a commission or consulting fee. We would recommend the customer add the 62.4 ounce purified and enhanced spring water for rinsing, as the natural chemical reaction of the two combined could double or triple the anti-aging effects, as verified in laboratory tests. This would be a must-have on top of a must-have on top of a must-have. The driver turned with a jerk, trying to miss a sudden dip, and my head banged into the window next to me. My daydream came to an abrupt end.

"Look," Fran said, pointing. I looked at the side of the road.

A young boy, maybe six or seven-years-old at the most, was riding a bike much too big for him. He carefully maneuvered around puddles, carrying four or more empty plastic milk jugs in each hand without letting go of the handlebars. Perhaps the recent rain had presented a new source of drinking water. Or perhaps he was simply carrying out a daily chore. In any case, the chances of finding any clean water nearby seemed small. The spinning back tire had already splattered a thick trail of mud up his legs, the length of his back, and into his hair. As it dried, it became gradually lighter, the color of coffee with a heavy dose of cream. What I had pictured as three shades darker than the skin of my imaginary customers was suddenly three shades lighter than the skin of this young water bearer. The contrast of browns was striking.

He rode past a house where a woman worked to push mud across the threshold of her home with a broom. Mud-soaked belongings rested on the patch of grass leading to the road. Her sandals did nothing to keep her feet protected, and the brown cascaded up her calves, growing lighter as it thinned and dried on her skin. After more miles of silence the isolation of the woman and the boy and the distance from the last village became more noticeable. Then we came upon the cooperative.

We tried carefully to keep our shoes clean as we walked across a piece of wood positioned between the truck and the entrance. The sun was setting quickly. A woman who appeared to be a manager eagerly turned on a bare light bulb to combat the darkness. We wiped our feet the best we could as we entered. A rainbow of handcrafted items graced the walls, behind the artisans sitting shyly in folding chairs. I wondered how close by they lived and how difficult it must be for them to return home in the dark. As much as I was taken by their work, my eyes turned to their faces. We listened attentively as our guide described the process of production.

"There has been some interest in distributing their goods in the U.S.," she noted, commenting on the need to teach the women what was actually more marketable there. Some discussion of the goods continued, as if they were things separate from the women sitting before us. Distinct. But I could almost see threads of light connecting the creations with the women. It is rare that we see creator and creation in one place at one time, and I wanted to see what had come from whom. There were similarities, bringing to mind a bit of mass production. Either one woman had produced many placemats, for example, with slight differences in decoration, or many women were taught to follow a pattern, producing a supply of each with her own special touches. And many of the items were completely unique.

There were household objects, decorative and functional, similar to some fair trade pieces available in other regions of underdeveloped Latin America. The paintings and sculptures were beautiful. But I was drawn to the items that reflected the essentials of living. They provided a sense of connection that transcended borders, class divisions, and races. I decided on an apron made of bright pink, soft, cotton broadcloth with calico accents. It had a bib and straps, and was gathered at the waist, reminding me of a childhood pinafore once given to me by my grandmother's sister, minus the ruffles at the shoulders. An embroidered "Haiti" graced the chest. I knew that I would wear it to cook. The universality of women and food preparation would bring the importance of family and nourishment to mind once back home. When I pointed to the apron and it was taken from the wall, one of the women beamed with delight. She swelled with a humble satisfaction and I knew then that she had made it.

We were reminded that dinner at the bishop's house awaited us, so we paid for our selections and were on our way. John took a photo of the women, a copy of which I have resting on the window ledge of my office at the university. It is a gentle reminder to me that women are women and work is work. I create course syllabi for my classes and they create aprons. And we all create meals. And I am grateful to have met them.

The apron hangs in my closet, and I do wear it from time to time. The holiday at home with the most elaborate family meal is Thanksgiving and wearing the apron invokes recognition of the abundance we have, as well as the waste and excess consumption that is so much a part of our lives. I prefer to wear it on not so special days as a reminder of the everyday fundamental need to feed oneself and one's children. I try not to think about how out of place the pink looks in a subdued beige suburban kitchen, or that tying it too snugly makes my hips look big. Rather, I try to wear it when making something "a la the Islands" such as beans and rice, or the occasional pumpkin dish. Pumpkin pie always goes down more sweetly when my pink apron is on especially knowing the distinctive place pumpkins hold for Haitians.

On the first of January, their Independence Day, Haitians traditionally eat pumpkin soup. The most important annual holiday, marking the beginning of a new nation and of a new year, it overshadows even Christmas, as there is little chance of splurging on gifts for friends and family. Under the colonial plantation system, pumpkins (indigenous to the

Americas) were restricted to the elite class. The vast majority of land was used to cultivate sugar for export and there was little concern for providing variety in the slaves' diets. Upon independence, the coveted pumpkin became a symbol of independence and freedom and pumpkin soup a traditional dish of commemoration. Wearing a pink apron while making pumpkin soup is a personal act of liberation perhaps meaningful only to me. Sometimes I am tempted to give history lessons to my friends and family, but I was fine keeping this one to myself.

13
Madonnas

Leaving Fort Liberté was not easy as we had made friends there. In my earlier years of travel I assumed I would make return trips to places that made a mark on me. By this time I knew that happens rarely, and only with intentional effort. As much as I wanted to see the area and its people again, I admitted I might never return.

Following our experiences with country life, Port-au-Prince seemed even more crowded and bustling than before. It was like any urban area, but with considerably more people per block out on the streets, doing whatever it is they have to do. With little electricity, even in the capital, they live mainly with the rhythm of the earth's rotation, activity substantially subsiding when the sun goes down, making the neighborhoods far quieter.

One evening, Jennifer, a Catholic Relief Services worker who had organized and led a number of our meetings in the city, asked if we would like to go for drink at a local bar. A few of us agreed. I was still not accustomed to the night in Haiti, and it was very dark. We had generally continued conversations following late dinners, and then retired to our rooms. Maneuvering through the streets of Port-au-Prince was a very different story. The level of electricity consumption in the United States becomes more palpable in contrast when visiting the less developed world. Hotel rooms and other types of accommodations are more dimly lit, as are the hallways leading up to them. The streets outside are as well. Sometimes it is a matter of using fewer bulbs, most often low-wattage fluorescents, which cast a gray tint on the walls, fixtures, furniture, and Caucasian skin. Where infrastructure is lacking and municipal funding short, streets often go unlit. That was the case in front of this corner bar.

Looking forward to a locally brewed beer or yet another version of rum punch, we carefully stepped over broken pieces of concrete and avoided holes on our way from the truck to the entrance. Glancing ahead to make sure I was keeping up with the others, I noticed a young woman approaching. She was carrying various sculptures wrapped gently in newspaper and lined neatly in a cardboard box. Considering her size, they must have weighed heavily on her forearms and hips. A very young girl, presumably her daughter, accompanied her. I had wanted to buy some art, preparing for a search sometime midweek, and here it was coming to me. The woman held up what looked like a soft stone carving of a mother and child. It was simple and graceful. She wanted 20 dollars. Before I could open my purse, Jennifer intervened, saying something in Creole. It took a moment to figure out what was happening. Then I nodded. The haggling had begun.

I have never been good at haggling. The only time I did it even close to effectively was in once in Cancún. It was more of a game there, with shop owners selling virtually the same thing in store after store. My kids looked on as I laughed along with my fellow hagglers, ending up with souvenirs that we certainly could have done without. Here, on a dark, empty street in Port-au-Prince I was more than willing to pay 20 dollars for this work of art from a frail craftswoman on my way into a bar. The statue began to take on some special significance as a Madonna, representing the woman and daughter herself, as well as the many others who populated the country. I looked at it more closely. It really was beautiful.

My Great Aunt Jeannette gave me a Madonna statue as a gift on the day I made my First Communion. It stood about ten inches tall and resembled the larger representations that adorned churches. To have something like it of my own made me feel even holier than I already did that day. I gave her a special place on my dresser and have since moved it with me wherever life has led.

Aunt Jeannette never had children and I later learned that she had very much wanted to. Knowing that about her made her own collection of Madonnas more fascinating to me. Having lost her husband many years before, she moved in with my grandmother when I was a young girl. She was very particular and her room was off-limits, except by personal invitation, making it somehow more mysterious and magical. Madonnas in various forms – statues, cards, small paintings – graced her room, as did a stemmed, cut-glass candy dish perpetually filled with lemon drops. Her walls and bed covering were of medium blues, as if she were veiled in the very colors of Mary herself. I imagined one day being old like her, still putting on lipstick every day, and having a blue room of my own with a jar filled with lemon drops.

Once as a young mother, when Katie was around 2-years-old, I spent an August day strolling through the Indian Market in Santa Fe. I was studying the American West, and the marvels of New Mexico had inspired a visit. Determined to purchase a remembrance on a graduate student's budget, I found a very small, hand-sewn doll made of cotton and deerskin. She wore a blue shawl and a red head scarf, and carried a baby. Katie did show interest in her for a time, but as is the case with most toys in our culture, she was eventually cast aside. Admitting she meant more to me than to my daughter, I decided to find a special place for safekeeping. I put her on my dresser, leaning against my Madonna. They could not have been more different in material and design, but I saw the connection instantly. There is something incredibly universal about a three-dimensional depiction of a mother and child. I saw it again quite vividly in the hands of the Haitian woman on that dark night.

"Would you pay 10 dollars?" Jennifer asked.

"Ten is fine," I told her.

"Nine," she told the woman. The woman agreed. I fished nine dollars from my wallet; she wrapped the statue in tissue and carefully handed it to me. We continued into the bar. I wanted to ask why Jennifer insisted on paying only nine, but figured she was much more experienced with this than I was. It was her third or fourth year living and working in Port-au-Prince.

On our way out that night we had met at Jennifer's home, where I was a bit taken aback by her situation. She lived in a compound of sorts, protected by a locked gate the width of the driveway and a security guard. I was surprised to learn that a worker for Catholic Relief Services would feel the need to be so protected. But she was a young woman living alone, so I suppose it made sense. The house was good-sized, even by U.S. standards, and posh by Haitian standards. It was the kind of house I wanted to have, and I am not one who covets much of anything. It was filled with art, unusual and striking. Absolutely filled. White outside and in, its walls were covered with paintings of every imaginable color, clearly by the same artist. She said he was a friend. They were busy and abstract, swirling in ways that words cannot describe, and just perfect.

In that moment, my Midwestern suburban life seemed more mundane than ever. I was in the middle of gutting my own house, cleansing and minimalizing everything about it in an effort to begin anew, post-divorce. I vowed to paint my own walls white when I returned home. I did. But I had very little art to hang, at least comparatively so, and it became as minimalist as minimalist could be. Still, I kept vivid memories of what she had done for her home.

The vestibule of the bar we visited was dark, but through a door draped with a grass curtain, a more well-lit and well-populated space lay inside. It was one of those indoor-outdoor structures common in warmer parts of the world. Once seated on stools, we saw that we were in fact outdoors, or in some sort of atrium. Atria are my favorite kinds of spaces, especially where plants abound. Not in malls and such, but in unexpected places. Libraries, for example.

In this Haitian pub, actually more a club, the sense was different. It was night time, making the whole idea of an atrium null. The sun did not drip in, rather the dim electric light escaped upward into the night sky. I have never understood much about the physics of light, but it seems that light flows out through spaces, much like liquid does, thinning and dispersing what is left behind. The club appeared darker than it might have if there were a proper ceiling. And artificial light, however little there is, obscures starlight and moonlight, so any effects they might have had were lost on us. We were left with a grayness that was neither inviting nor imposing. It was just there. Some young men came by to introduce themselves. They were friends of Jennifer, or friends of friends. I ordered a rum punch.

Two men in particular seemed so very muscular. White, American, and muscular. Bulked. I was told they had been Marines and were now working as security guards for Aristide. He had been elected again and was serving his second term in office. I heard more than one person comment in the days before that he was spending an astronomical amount of money on security. Once actually in the country I had hoped to learn more about Aristide from Haitians living in Haiti. But when I raised the topic, no matter how carefully, I felt a sense of tension and a lack of willingness to talk openly. That was the case here, as well. There did not seem to be room for a free exchange of ideas about the nuances or extremes in political ideology or practices, or anything in between. What was said I did not understand, making me realize there was far more to the situation than I could have imagined. I did not push for information.

I took the Madonna from the paper wrapping and showed the others. Her arms were smooth and cool and cradled an infant at her breast. They liked it very much. And I knew she would look just right in her own special place on my dresser.

Before we left Port-au-Prince we did find some time to explore artists' work displayed along the streets, in the daylight. I wanted to purchase a painting. Many of them looked very similar to one another and we were told to assume they may be mass-produced. But there were plenty that stood out as wonderfully unique and captivating. I chose one portraying two faces of the same woman, one a profile and the other staring directly forward. Her skin was rich in several shades of brown, both sets of lips full and red. She was cloaked in orange, pink, green, yellow, and lavender, positioned to resemble a blossoming flower against a blue sky. Her dark eyes opened to the depths of her mind, looking ahead and not down.

For years, I carried around the canvas, promising one day to have it suitably framed to hang in my living room. And I finally did. She now looks over me, a reminder of my gratitude for having had the opportunity to see her homeland. And she is notably without children or even a body that might produce children. Even mothers of children deserve to be reminded that they are women first, women who can stand alone.

14
Orphanages

Even though I had warned Tom that I did not want to visit any orphanages I knew the day would come when I had to go along. My heart was still pretty fragile and I was afraid it might break. But I could not very well stay behind. Port-au-Prince has hundreds of orphanages. It is a way of life for many. Children are often left without parents due to AIDS or other diseases and many times their parents are alive but unable to care for them.

The first one we visited had been started by a priest who one day found a baby left on his doorstep. There was nothing he could do but take care of the child. Once word of his kindness spread other babies began appearing on his doorstep. By 2003, he was able to organize a staff and acquire a large house, where they cared for more than 40 children.

The house was white and children greeted us on the front steps. They smiled excitedly at the sight of visitors and pulled on our hands to help us inside. Light poured into the living area which was full of toys and books. They wanted to show us everything. A few of the others in our group seemed more comfortable, apparently more experienced in such visits. As I watched them at ease with the children I felt someone tugging at my knee. He was a boy of around two, wearing a red t-shirt and soft khaki pants. He looked up at me and put his arm around my leg as if we went together. We stood there while the others mixed and mingled. We were told that human touch was something the children had come to crave, and he held on so tight I could not walk. My head told me to pick him up and carry him over to the sofa, but my own issues with human touch seemed to be standing in the way.

Months had passed since the man I had fallen in love with moved to California, and I still missed his touch. Sam, my youngest, thank goodness was still open to hugs. Danny and Katie were teens and hugged less frequently and more reluctantly. Looking down I realized I could probably use some more good human touch myself. I peeled one of his hands from my pant leg. He would not let go with the other, but it was enough for me to hobble to the other side of the room with him attached so I could sit down. He continued to lean in as close as he could, never letting go of my leg. I continued to watch the others, but he never took his eyes off me. I learned that he had been brought there as an infant severely malnourished, which placed him far below normal weight. His size had eventually reached average, but his cognitive development had not quite caught up.

The other children moved quickly around the room showing off what they could do with balls and blocks, the common language being smiles. I picked up the boy, placed him on my lap, and put my arms around him. He melted back into me, letting me know he was a perfect fit. I wanted to let him know this would last only a minute, and wondered if this kind of meeting with attaching and letting go of strangers was a common occurrence in his life.

When it was time to leave, I stood up and planted his feet firmly on the floor. His arms rewound tightly at my knee. As I attempted to walk toward the door, one of the staff members worked gently to help him let go. I reluctantly turned to say good-bye and his eyes met mine. They seemed to say that he was ok with parting. Or maybe that is what I wanted them to say. In any case, I was ok with it. More ok than I had predicted. The experience made me more conscious of how often people come in and out of our lives, often there for only a very short time. Within the intersection there may be meaning, purpose. It might happen at a sales counter or in a restaurant, at the circulation desk of a library, or on a city sidewalk. The need for some sort of exchange brings two people together, even if we do not fully understand at the time what it is. Sometimes all we can do is to acknowledge it and offer eye contact and a smile. That is what the boy and I gave to each other before I walked back down the steps. There was nothing more we could do. Whew, I thought. Not so bad. One orphanage down. Three to go.

The next was easier. There were no children there at the time of our visit, as they were away on a field trip of some kind. We had traveled high into the hills above the city center and the space available for the children there was incredible. So was the view. The meals provided were essentially based on a grain mixture provided by the United States, very common in institutions serving children. It was stored in large plastic drums and mixed with water at meal time, providing basic sustenance. The sleeping areas were stark, with metal triple bunks lining the walls. Again, only what was needed. I imagined children filling the rooms at bedtime.

Outdoors there was a vast green space with a play area and trees, and what seemed to be a pretty decent basketball court. The universality of basketball always strikes a chord in me, especially in a place so far from home. Particularly sweet was the Chicago Bulls backboard. Traveling inevitably inspires discussions of origins as it brings people together from distant places. Though Indiana gave birth to individuals like Cole Porter, James Dean, and Eugene Debs, it is unlikely that people from other countries identify them as Hoosiers or can even locate the state on a mental map. And because the Calumet Region lies in the most northwest corner of the state and exists more as a part of the Chicago metropolitan area, those of us from there often simply tell people we meet that we are from Chicago. Much of the rest of the state's inhabitants would like us to secede anyway, as our Democratic politics and continued position as a union stronghold make us so unlike the majority of them.

It has always been a bit unsettling that Chicago was so well-known in other parts of the world for being home to Al Capone, even decades after his escapades. Now it was refreshing to learn that Chicago was identified with Michael Jordan. Kids everywhere knew him, even here looking out over Port-au-Prince. I missed my boys. When Sam was born in 1992, Dan was turning four and had become a bigger Bulls fan than I imagined anyone could be at that age. He told me if the new baby was a boy, he wanted us to name him Michael Jordan Schlesinger. As much as we were fans, too, his father and I had to tell him that we probably would not do that. Now I wanted both my sons to be with me.

The next orphanage visit was far more challenging. It was one that housed strictly AIDS-infected babies – many dozens of them – and was run by the Missionaries of Charity. This is the order founded by Mother Teresa and they each resembled her in their dress and undying devotion and selfless service marking their work and demeanor. We took a few photos of the babies, but the sisters refused to be photographed, as doing so violated their vows. The youngest infants were housed two to a crib, and it was meal time when we arrived. Their cries turned into wails and we did our best to help keep them calm. Between the sisters and the members of our group, there was still only one of us for about every five or six babies. Any concern for the spread of AIDS disappeared, as the desperate need for comfort superseded.

The wails grew louder in room after room and feeding was the only thing that came close to calming them. And when it was not feeding that demanded our attention, it was changing diapers. We stepped up quickly to help the sisters – who never seemed to stop smiling – tend to one after another. As I tried to comfort one, I saw Carol put another back into a crib and walk outside. I followed her to see what had happened. She was in tears. It got to her. It got to me, too. One by one, the women in our group appeared outside. Deep breaths and silence were all we could muster. Anyone who has had to comfort a hungry, sick baby knows how heart-wrenching and exhausting it can be. The sisters dealt with this all day, every day, and suddenly their lives seemed something beyond my comprehension.

Without my knowing, John had taken a photo of me leaning over to rub the back of one of two babies in a crib. I am not a big fan of documenting every experience with photos, as has become so common now. For some, it seems to have reached the point that unless there is a photographic record, they have not really lived it. But John was there because the bishop was there. And having the orphanage photo on my desk reminds me of a day I might otherwise have not believed myself. It is said that we remember positive experiences in more detail than we do negative ones. If that is the case, I wonder why I remember that day at all. It must have been the sisters.

The last orphanage we visited was affiliated with

Montessori education. A Canadian woman began the project and ended up making it her life's work. It started small, as do many worthwhile undertakings, and grew impressively. The operation had recently moved into a very large, unoccupied home the size of a mansion. Property ownership, rights, and responsibilities are skewed in Haiti and often what is owned is left uncared for, unoccupied, and otherwise unused. The acquisition of land and buildings is a status symbol, and while much of the population remains poor, hungry, and homeless, there appears little guilt derived from failing to utilize soil or space for a greater social purpose.

The situation breeds some class conflict, sometimes nurtured by politicians but often emerging organically because of circumstances. It also breeds a disregard for ownership when practical, entrepreneurial people see a need and endeavor to put their ideas to work. This seemed the case with this school director. As her operation grew increasingly popular and successful it required a larger facility, and she, her staff, and students bravely "squatted" in the building. By the time we arrived, it appeared to serve wonderfully, its large rooms housing classes and office workers with simple beauty and efficiency. The rooms' walls were painted in warm hues of yellow and orange and decorated with messages of inspiration and students' work. Walking through them brought back the most soothing of memories of visiting my own elementary school during open houses, and those of my children. It was a happy place.

Katie, Dan, and Sam had each attended a Montessori school for at least a couple years in their early childhood, so I was familiar with its philosophy and methods. Students generally work independently at their own pace, making new discoveries in learning and expression. They are encouraged to be respectful of their environment, taking care of plants, for example, and being considerate of others. They work alone but for the good of the classroom community, and become curiously adept at subjects and skills related to mathematics, languages, sciences, geography, and culture. It was mesmerizing to observe the enthusiasm and devotion that this woman and her staff had brought to Port-au-Prince children. What was even more striking was the fact that each of the residents there was infected with HIV.

I looked carefully at each drawing and piece of writing decorating the hallways and classrooms, and found myself lagging behind as the group moved ahead. Soon I turned back toward what had been pointed out the nurse's office just off the main entrance. I was missing my children dearly, or I should say missing their younger days. Each one had ended up in their nurse's office at one time or another with a playground injury, a sudden fever, a real or imagined stomach ache, or congestion that I should not have ignored as I led them to school and then hurried off to work. Each episode tied me to them more tightly. Just feeling nostalgic, I suppose, and curious about the nurturing of a child back to health during a Port-au-Prince school day.

When I entered the room, there was a small bed in the corner, just as I had imagined, and a child snuggled under warm blankets. She looked no more than 3- or 4-years-old. She gazed up at me and smiled weakly. I recalled my own junior high days of feigning illness during an exam here and there, knowing now that I was fooling no one. She was too young to be faking it, I thought, but she seemed more at peace than in pain. Perhaps she was a bit drained that day, too hungry or tired to make it through the afternoon without a rest.

She squirmed from under the covers and looked as if

she wanted to talk. Another girl walked in and explained to me in Creole what was wrong with her friend – at least that is what I imagined. She seemed to try it again in French, and I smiled at both of them. The friend standing next to me patted my arm and the sick girl's shoulder. She then took my hand and placed it on the girl and smiled. Soon the covers were inching down and arms stretched out for a hug. The length of her reach stunned me. As it became clear she wanted me to hold her, I let her hands grasp the back of my neck while I attempted to pick her up. Her hips and legs were frighteningly thin, and I suddenly realized she had to be 9- or 10-years-old, more than four and a half feet tall, though maybe only 60 pounds. She was not a preschooler at all. She held on to me with the little strength she had, and her friend watched with love. Then, much to my surprise, the girl had a bowel movement so loose that it ran through her clothing and dripped down my arm. I do not recall shrieking, but I must have let out a cry of some kind. She pressed her cheek into my chest as her friend ran from the room for help.

A staff member entered, ran out, and then returned with a bundle of cotton and what appeared to be rubbing alcohol. She gently took the girl from my arms, placed her back on the bed and then turned her attention to me. Resources of any kind are scarce across the country, but she seemed to spare no expense in cleaning me up. Handful after handful of cotton was drenched in alcohol and wiped across my skin. She carefully examined my clothing but it was clean. It turned out that the girl was in the later stages of AIDS and near death. It had become customary in this school for the children to learn age-appropriate truths about AIDS and have afflicted and dying classmates nearby. It was the intention of the school director to make sure students comprehended what was happening.

AIDS was widespread in Haiti, and there was still much misunderstanding surrounding it.

In my first few years out of college during the early 1980s, AIDS was spreading in the United States, accompanied by fear, paranoia, and hateful discrimination. Not until teenager Ryan White from Kokomo, Indiana died was there much realistic acceptance of people who had contracted it. The fear in Haiti was accompanied by voodoo sentiments suggesting that a curse could cause someone to become ill and with little understanding of how it was spread entire villages might shun the afflicted. It sounds extreme, but in fact not all that different from the way in which people in the United States were deemed cursed by God for their behavior, and shunned by society. Here, some 20 years later, Haitian children were being accepted by one another and taught, through their unique exposure to the effects of AIDS, that death was a part of life. This was a far cry from how my own children might learn of death. Here it was much closer, and more real.

I did shower extra thoroughly upon returning to my room later, wondering myself just what level of risk I had encountered by hugging the girl. A more or less faithful blood donor, I knew just being in Haiti banned me from donating for at least a year, and by then I would be sure it was safe. I was not in a sexual relationship at the time, which eased my mind. And, I thought, if I did become infected, so be it. But I did not. Knowing so brought a sense of relief. Still, I will never forget the girl's face or the love shared through the face of her friend.

15
THE MASS

Attending Mass in other countries helps to illuminate the concept of the Catholic Church as something universal. The languages are different but the ritual is the same. The architectures of the sanctuaries are different but the elements are the same. There is something both peculiar and familiar about Catholic churches that are not your own. The surrounding town and the parishioners are different. But there is something constant about it. There are many things similar in Paris, Guatemala, or Chicago. And it was the case in Haiti, as well.

The bishop celebrated the Mass with translation all week, and on this particular day he did so in a church that felt very old and comforting. It was tall, with a choir loft above and behind, and painted a warm cream, the color of white peaches. The pews were hard and the parishioners reserved. As a chronic people-watcher, the service provided me the perfect opportunity to observe Haitian behavior. Parents' toward children, children's toward parents, community members' toward one another. Two things struck me most. First, the perfection of the "Sunday best" which every person wore. In a place where living conditions are so poor it is difficult to imagine the care it would take to look so wonderful for Mass. Second, the widespread mannerisms of humility were especially apparent. Perhaps they were accentuated under the circumstances, or perhaps I had taken more time to notice. Haitians keep their eyes low and their hands close to their bodies. That may seem a blatant generalization, but in comparison to others of the islands or of the Americas, it is noticeable.

I find myself visiting churches when traveling, as others might visit cemeteries or tequila bars. They are fascinating to me. But only on occasion have I taken the opportunity to attend Mass. A few months earlier while participating in an Irish Studies conference in St. Louis I was told there was an interesting church down the street from my hotel, one worthy of a visit. It reportedly was filled with tile mosaics, floor to ceiling. It was just a short walk away and the conference had come to an end by Sunday morning, so I had no excuses. This was at one of those times when Mass seemed to be in order. Feeling alienated from love and my work, I wanted to retreat into the young Kathy who found solace in the Mass.

The church was indeed beautiful, unlike any I had ever seen. The mosaic tile was intricately detailed and seemingly infinite. It began in the vestibule, where I paused, captivated. Then I entered. I crossed myself with holy water, its coolness dripping from the center of my forehead and peppering my jacket. I genuflected and sat in in a pew located in the center right, not too far but not too close, for this was not my church. Even in my own I still felt like a guest and here in a city new to me, I did even more so. The rhythm, the ritual, and the passive calm it brought to me, were familiar. It is sometimes those things which critics point to as symbols of routine in Catholic services. But more often than not, they are exactly what I am looking for.

The structure itself was large, old, and full of echoes, so unlike my circa 1970, carpeted, earth-toned, post-Vatican II comfort zone. It was reminiscent of my second-home church, St. Joseph's, where my grandparents attended and my parents were married. That, too, was large, old, and full of echoes and wooden, unpadded kneelers – the kind just right for doing penance. But the St. Louis Mass was different in one remarkable respect. The priest, during his sermon, spoke about the pending war in Iraq, and not in a favorable way. There he stood, high behind a lectern of wood and marble surrounded by meticulously pieced designs – a setting that could not have been more solid, stable, or conservative, I thought – jutting up and out as if positioned between us and heaven. I had heard countless sermons in my life, and very few had ever acknowledged anything occurring in present time and place. Providing background on the conflict, his comments were enlightening and I agreed very much with him that the direction the U.S. government had taken was dangerous on many levels. My memories turned to the student interested in voodoo who had heard sermons from his pastor which crassly mixed history with religion, and I wondered if there was much difference. Yes there was. What this priest was saying was true for me.

While we were in Haiti, the war was even more imminent. In the Department du Nord-Est we could not have felt further from a climate of hi-tech and oil-driven aggression. On our last evening there, we sat in the living room area, more of a parlor or drawing room, at the Fort Liberté bishop's house where we were staying. He had been a remarkable host, and it was intriguing to watch him interact with his peer, our bishop. It was January of 2003, and George Bush was on the television. Here, so far from home, with such limited contact with the outside world, it was surreal to see the U.S. President. The privileged lifestyle of the bishop allowed for relaxing accommodations, yet another feast of a meal, and now CNN. Those of us in the group had talked of politics along the way and though our perspectives differed on various points, there had been a common frustration with the President and the way he was carrying out foreign policy. We could not be sure of the true role he was playing, as it appeared clearly orchestrated by the people surrounding him. And at this point we were coming closer every day to an attack on Iraq.

Being outside the country when the U.S. government is behaving badly can be awkward to say the least. The behavior exhibited in early 2003 was nothing less than embarrassing and often infuriating. The bishop graciously served us after dinner liqueurs from a beautiful tray and we began to discuss world affairs. The incandescent light warmed the soft buttery yellow walls even more, reminding me of a gathering room at my grandmother's church when I was a young girl. Heavy dark brown woodwork and the scent of beeswax candles took me back. I was also reminded of the presidential speeches of my early youth. My parents never missed a broadcast of John F. Kennedy. We sat close to the television and through his words tried to make sense of the adult world. Listening to Bush made me realize just how jaded I had become. I did not believe what he was saying and wondered if even he believed it. I did not like where his administration was taking the country and how its steps were affecting the world. The north of Haiti seemed so isolated, so insulated, with daily needs detached from global practices, I thought. But I knew that was not the case and at that moment it was difficult to call myself an American.

"We like Americans, we just don't like your government's policies," I had been told repeatedly in conversations with

Europeans and Latin Americans. I had grown grateful for their sentiment but not completely satisfied. After all, if this is anything close to a democracy, are we not responsible for our government? Our Haitian hosts knew that perhaps no one in the room had voted for Bush. A significant number of Catholics visiting Haiti included progressives committed to peace and justice. And the bishop did not hesitate to criticize the Bush administration's approach to foreign affairs. When it became clear he was in like-minded company, he retreated to the adjoining room where there was a computer. He had printed a copy of Bush's State of the Union Address, and quoted from it. It was filled with fear mongering and essentially said that he would take action regardless of what the United Nations advised.

I realized just what far-reaching effects this would have on the world. In the past there had been numerous acts on the part of the United States directed at Haiti and surrounding territories. Though protested by some, at the time they were rationalized. As time went by, public outcry grew. Those who studied the history of U.S. foreign policy honestly acknowledged similarities in current developments. On this occasion, when it appeared U.S. policy had nothing to do with Haiti, the reaction there was clear. To engage in war without provocation was reminiscent of past actions and an affront to all who respected peace. The bishop of Fort Liberté expected more from the world's most powerful leaders.

Two months later, the United States followed through on its threats to attack Iraq. My daughter and some friends had spoken out against the war in her high school, as did some colleagues and I on my campus. We argued with reason why this was a mistake politically, economically, and morally. We were by no means the most vocal of the pending war's critics, but our position was clear. When the attack finally did take place, I had resigned myself to the fact that the Bush administration simply could not be deterred. Katie, on the other hand, was demoralized in a way that only an 18-year-old could be.

The following day she asked if I would take her shopping for a prom dress after dinner. She was not obsessed with prom, but it was her senior year and she looked forward to going with a friend. He was a great guy, very smart, and hilarious, and I knew they would have a good time. It was still some time away and we were in no hurry to get a dress, but she was scheduled to leave the following morning along with her brothers to spend spring break in Palm Springs with their grandparents. It almost seemed like a task she wanted to check off her to-do list, but I also think she wanted to get the war off her mind. I agreed to take her for a quick trip into the city, thinking we could just get some idea about styles and how much this was going to set me back. I also decided that her brothers were old enough to be home by themselves for a few hours, knowing that their father and my mother were nearby.

It was good to be in the car alone with her. Time can slip away and I had heard that car rides with one child at a time give parents a chance to talk and listen, and she was more or less captive. By the time we reached Soldier Field, we had touched on a good variety of topics. But it was clear she was still pretty downhearted. After some time of sitting in stopped traffic, I realized something was wrong. We were at a complete standstill. Several black, unmarked police cars sped north on the road's shoulder, next to us. I could not imagine what kind of emergency had befallen the downtown area.

When we finally heard on the radio that protesters had taken Lake Shore Drive, Katie came to life.

"Mom! I want to go find them!" she pleaded.

I had heard there would be a demonstration if there were indeed an attack on Iraq but had forgotten about it. Joining a protest that evening could not have been further from my mind.

"Katie, we've got to get home early. It's a school night and your brothers are home alone."

"Please? Please, Mom?" The thought of anti-war activists not giving up seemed to lend her some kind of hope. I gave in.

"Just for a little while. We came here to look for a prom dress."

"All right, I promise."

We parked the car near Water Tower Place and I took only my keys, driver's license, and Marshall Field's credit card with me. By that time the group had reached the area in front of the Drake Hotel. Within minutes I saw a young man hit and being dragged by police. I did not want Katie to be a witness to this and feared for her safety. I took her arm and led her away.

"We're getting out of here," I told her. When we reached Michigan Avenue a line of police in riot gear blocked the sidewalk. I took her back to the other side of the hotel, but police obstructed us there, as well. I pleaded with them to let us go but they refused.

We had no choice but to join the protesters as they were led by police back down Lake Shore Drive and onto Chicago Avenue. I was relieved, as we were closer to our car. But police three-deep surround us. One by one they slowly arrested people who did nothing more than stand there. After an hour or two of asking them to let us leave I heard Katie scream.

"Mom!" I turned around to see her being taken by police.

"Wait!" I yelled. "Take me with her! She's my daughter!"

We were put into a paddy wagon and eventually locked up with hundreds of others. She and I were separated into different cells. I could not imagine how she was handling the situation and ached to be with her.

I later learned that initially she had found a sense of camaraderie with her cell mates, but by the following day had broken down and curled up in the fetal position on the cold, cement floor, sobbing. She was finally brought into my cell, where we were confined with others until late the following night.

I am not sure what prompted me to join the protesters that night, but I spent a good deal of the time behind bars remembering our visit with the bishop in Fort Liberté, who was so saddened by President Bush's stance.

16
CRISES

Following the 2003 visit to Haiti, I very much looked forward to returning. It was draining and I wondered how non-Haitians spent so much of their lives there, but I knew there was something between Haiti and me that was not quite finished. However, the next trip would be delayed. Just a year later, Haiti was in turmoil. The violence against the Aristide administration had grown to unprecedented proportions. We had been warned for some time by Catholic Relief Services that tensions were growing, making a return trip unlikely for some time. I underestimated the tensions, and thought the group organizers were being overprotective. It is true that hosting visitors detracts from their own work, so I suspected that a subsequent delegation might be too much to take on for a while. They truly felt responsible for us, and perhaps traveling with the bishop intensified their efforts. But they assured us that they would be happy for us to return sometime later when it was safe. They kindly reiterated that they knew best and had our interests at heart.

In coming months, news of political violence swept news channels and it became increasingly apparent that they had known something we did not. Haiti would not make the news if this had not been a major development. The violence this time was different from what I had heard described before. Or perhaps it seemed so, because I was more familiar with the country, its geography, and its people than I had been. In Fort Liberté we had been strikingly close to the Dominican border, so when it was reported that armed Haitians were entering the country just south of there, I could picture it more vividly.

The images finally available on news sites showed people with expensive garb and weaponry, indicating they were being outfitted from somewhere outside Haiti. The cynic in me suggested it might be the United States. After all, discontent seemed to be mounting in various areas in an effort to destabilize the entire country. It was possible the emergence was organic and homegrown but knowing what I did about the history of U.S.-Latin American relations it was also quite possibly influenced by non-Haitian players. Aristide was no friend of the Bush administration. Though Clinton had succeeded in assisting him to his rightful place in 1994, Aristide's relationship with the United States had grown sour under his second term in office.

The Haitian President's approach toward economic justice still appeared grounded in liberation theology, which to U.S. conservatives, especially fundamentalist Protestants, smacked of Left wing, socialist heresy. Following the attacks on the United States on September 11, 2001, Latin American terrorist watch lists grew and included countless left-leaning groups. Perhaps the Department of State felt it could not afford critics so close to home to maintain their status of legitimacy. By 2003, U.S. diplomats were working tirelessly to gain Latin American support for U.S. military efforts in Iraq.

Having studied more about the School of the Americas (SOA) in recent years (now called the Western Hemispheric Institute for Security Cooperation or WHINSEC) I wondered what role the U.S. military might have played in training Haitians to take armed control of their country. The SOA worked in counterinsurgency, not insurgency, training, but I did discover there was a branch in Missouri devoted to teaching courses in Haitian Creole. Historians do not speculate, I reminded myself. Unless I could take time to investigate my suspicions adequately, I should just stay away from the topic. Still, developments in Haiti were disturbing, especially now that I had become more intimately familiar with the country. I discussed my concerns with some colleagues. A few dismissed my fears while others confirmed my suspicions indicating there was probably even more to the story than I had considered.

I decided a campus presentation on the matter was in order and sought a guest speaker with some expertise through the Haitian Consulate in Chicago. The receptionist said the Consul General would be happy to see me, and scheduled an appointment for the following day. Attention to Haiti and work in general had taken my mind off my personal life, and that became more apparent as I made the trek downtown. Walking along State Street reminded me that there used to be a life for me outside the classroom, library, and attempts to keep my children's lives as stable and secure as possible. The bright sun made this other world populated by urban workers and retail shoppers more visible.

I stopped in a popular shop to buy some caramel corn. The aroma-laden air was warm and filled my mind with the simplicity of childhood memories. My father used to repair watches in his spare time and would sometimes bring us downtown with him to pick up watch parts. He never charged more than a dollar or two for his labor, so we were never quite sure what rewards it could have offered him. He spent many hours each week hunched over his workbench, eyepiece aiding in his view of the tiniest of mainsprings, watch stems, and crystals. He patiently let us observe him work, even when friends tagged along. Getting the watch parts he needed required trips to Jewelers' Row in the Loop, for which he preferred a car ride to the El, and the El to South Wabash. When we accompanied him, we would beg to stop for caramel corn. He agreed only rarely, as his method of parenting seemed to rely far more on creating simple experiences of being together than of buying us things. Walking ever so slowly past the caramel corn shop and sticking our faces into the doorway to get a whiff would usually have to suffice.

On my walk back to the car from the Consulate after securing a speaker, I smelled caramel corn. The child in me needed a treat and the adult in me was convinced it would not break the budget. So, caramel corn it was. It would help sweeten an otherwise difficult time in my life, or so I thought. When I returned home, I left on the kitchen counter what I had not eaten and before bed Sam finished it. I was pleased to share the experience of downtown Chicago sweetness, even if he had not been able to accompany me on this trip.

The next day's morning routine stress magnified exponentially as Sam exited his bedroom and met me in the hall.

"I can't breathe," he rasped.

"What? Your voice sounds terrible. I didn't know you were catching a cold." I went on getting ready for work in one of those mom states of mind where I made medical decisions based on my demands at work.

"Mom, I can't breathe." He sat down on the stairs and looked an ashen gray. Oh, my God, I could say only in my mind. I worked desperately to prevent my sudden panic from panicking him. And my knife-like sharpness of mothering instinct became jumbled with stupidity.

"Do you have an inhaler?" My mind turned to the caramel corn, which must have contained nuts, which must have triggered this. His allergy/asthma attacks were rare, and we had become lax about having antihistamines and albuterol around.

"I think there's one at Dad's." His dad lived nearby, but going there on the hope he had an inhaler would have taken just as long as a run to the store, and would likely have been accompanied by unnecessary comments regarding my qualifications as a mother.

"Wait here," I said, as I took off for the one drugstore I knew would be open before 7:30 a.m. Though he was 11-years-old, he looked to me like a toddler as I ran out the door. About six blocks from my house I heard the siren of a police car and saw its flashing lights in my rear view window. No, it couldn't be. I looked down at my speedometer and realized I had quickly reached twenty miles over the speed limit. After pulling over and seeing him park behind me, I jumped out and ran toward him. In retrospect, this was not a smart move.

"Ma'am, stop!" The patrol officer jumped from his car. "You don't do that!"

"My son is having an asthma attack and I'm on my way to the drugstore!"

"Ma'am, you could cause an accident." I looked around and saw no other cars on the road. I thought it not a good idea to point that out to him.

"I have to get to the drugstore!"

"Where is your son?" I have no idea why I did not bring with me, except that I wanted to keep him calm and home seemed the right place for that.

"At home." He let me go, but my heart was still racing as

he followed slowly, keeping me to the speed limit.

I reached the pharmacy, parked in the first spot I could find, and ran inside. The pharmacist was notably kind, diligently looking up records and asking the basic questions as quickly as she could. Maybe two hours, or five minutes, later, I ran back to my car. There was the officer, signing a ticket. I could not believe it. I said nothing, took the ticket, and got the inhaler to my son as fast as I possibly could. I then waited with gleeful anticipation for the opportunity to go to traffic court to fight injustice.

When my court date finally arrived, I sat patiently, quite full of myself in this gallant effort. This officer was in for one hell of a heavy-handed reprimand. I was sure of it. My name was called and I argued my case. A familiar looking couple of suited gentlemen sat near the judge, staring in a way that made me uneasy. This was my hometown, but since my marriage ended it seemed to be one in which divorced mothers were pariahs, so one which nearly killed her child with nut-laced caramel corn was apparently a menace to society. They said something I could not hear and then came the voice of the judge.

"Guilty," the judge said, in a manner that left no room for discussion.

"But, Your Honor—" I had to explain.

"You were driving on a suspended license, and apparently still are. The officer was being generous with you."

"Generous? Suspended license? How?"

"An unpaid ticket for a speeding violation in Kosciusko County last year." Oh jeez. I did get pulled over for speeding on my way back from Dan's basketball tournament in Fort Wayne. Taking the scenic route across the dullest and flattest part of the state with a carful of boys proved a bit too much and

I could not bring myself to stay within the speed limit.

"But I was never notified."

"Did you have a change of address?"

"Yes. I had to move on with my li—" I stopped. Too much information. "Yes, I moved across town."

"Traffic citations are not forwarded."

"How was I supposed to know that?" None of this made sense. And how was this cop looking like the good guy here?

"One hundred and eighty five dollars." I wondered where the hell I was going to get a hundred and eighty five dollars. This was reminding me far too much of the time I had to come up with money to bail Katie and myself out of jail in Chicago.

Oh my God. That had to appear on my record. No wonder I was not getting a break. At this point my record must have looked like that of no other mother in Munster, Indiana. The charges had been dropped after subsequent court appearances, but perhaps there was some way it remained in the computer's database. I don't remember how I came up with the one hundred eighty five dollars to pay the traffic ticket, but I did. Resourcefulness had become one of my strongest traits, as did faith things would all work out in the end.

Reconciling my worldview, professional dedication, and commitment to global affairs with my suburban mom life seemed to become harder rather than easier as time went by. But what got me through was remembering the very basics of life itself which transcended cultural and national boundaries – a mother's love for her children, the prospects for having a home, the desire for peace. And in some strange way I was grateful that I had not become accustomed to the comforts of American life, and all its glories. Because it did not bring me satisfaction I found it easier to strip its elements away, and find common ground with people who in all respects might seem so unlike me. In fact, I often felt more in common with the women of Haiti than I did with women of my own town.

What mostly remains of the caramel corn memory is the awareness of my yearning to protect my own child from the terror of an asthma attack and the broken-heartedness of divorce that surrounded his life. What remains of the jail memories is my daughter's disillusionment with her country's leaders, and my inability to shield her from a terrifying experience. I tried to do what I could to see the experience through her eyes. We had not done anything wrong, and it hurt me beyond words to see her like that. I wondered how women in much more dire situations were able to shelter their children from harm that comes their way.

17
LEARNING

When I reminisce about particular classes, memories of seating positions, desk arrangements and flooring come to mind, in addition to students. It was rare that one of my classes was scheduled in room 342, so that semester's History of the Caribbean setting is more vivid. The room differed distinctly from the others. It must have been 2005 or 2006, for that was when I met Renate and it was a joy to invite her as a guest speaker. My classroom was laid out like a very small lecture hall, with angled stationary tables and tiered rows. The carpet and soft wall covering made the space feel more intimate, and though it was difficult to move students around for small group work, we were able to get to know each other well.

To the center right in the first row sat three young women who were majoring in education. They were nearing graduation and becoming excited about the prospects of teaching. They brought a dynamic sensitivity regarding social and cultural issues to their work and to the classroom. Their endless curiosity and commitment to learning was remarkable, as was their determination to make the world a better place through teaching. Each in their own way they made me come to know how any small thing I added to their education might be magnified one hundred fold, in a good way. The experience helped me become more aware of the thread that connects teachers teaching teachers teaching teachers teaching teachers. For that I am eternally grateful.

Neither they nor I saw education as simply a matter of transferring a core of information from one head to another. Rather, we knew it to be a never ending process on the parts of both teacher and student. I have always felt that my primary responsibility in teaching was to continue my journey of discovery and invite others to join me. I had met these students before and was so happy to see that they had chosen to be part of the journey of discovering the Caribbean. They each stayed in touch, and I loved when they shared their teaching experiences with me. The directions they took seemed profound and far beyond any help I might have provided. It is possible for students to view professors as somewhat greater creatures than they really are. I looked back on some of the teachers who inspired me and have since seen more of their humanness.

Also in that class was Heleine. When she spoke, I noticed an accent.

"Where are you from?" I asked her during the first week of class. Those of us in multicultural studies feel free to ask what others might not dare to or care to. I am fascinated by immigration and how and why people have come to be where they are, and I am especially intrigued by accented blacks in the United States. African Americans comprise the oldest of our immigrant groups next to the English, so their integration – or lack thereof – is part of a long, long, story. However, voluntary migration from Africa is very new, essentially taking place only since the Immigration and Nationality Act of 1965 which removed quotas favoring northern and western Europeans. To have an accent means a physical move, and rather than a distant and detached immigration history, somewhere in each there is an individual and personal migration story.

My curiosity about Heleine's accent and what her story might be was piqued. I wondered what our semester together would hold. Perhaps she was from West Africa and could add priceless insight as we uncovered the story of the Atlantic slave trade. Or it could be East Africa making her therefore detached from this and confronting our assumptions that all blacks in the U.S. hold some connection to the history of New World slavery. Or what if, I imagined, she were from the Caribbean? What an asset her presence would be – a definite opportunity to keep me on my toes.

"Haiti," she replied. That is not what I expected. And I could not have imagined a better gift. Her manner was modest and her voice kind; common, I was coming to know, among Haitians. She seemed honored to be in the class, but I could not have been more honored myself to have her as a student.

Her family came to the United States when she was a teenager, and settled in Florida. It was during the tumultuous 1980s as Baby Doc was being ousted from power. She met her husband in the United States, and they raised three children together. He was white, a lawyer I believe, and his work brought them to Indiana, where they settled. She mentioned he was white before I met him, I suppose thinking I needed to be prepared. It didn't matter, except that it made an otherwise interesting story even more so. Over the years we came to know each other better, and once over lunch we commiserated about raising teenagers in suburban America. But her experiences held an added dimension. She described how frustrating it was to have daughters who took their privileges for granted. She laughed as she explained how her own daily life during childhood had demanded a good deal of physical labor – much of it in the form of carrying things – carrying large containers of fresh milk, jugs of water, baskets of laundry, and so on. Her children, born in the United States, were typical but the cultural chasm between them and their mother compared with that between my children and me, was far greater.

Listening to her reminded me of an amazing conversation I once had with an Ethiopian taxi driver in Minneapolis. He lamented the difficulties of getting his teenaged, American-born son to sit down to dinner with the family. After describing the scarcity of sustenance during his upbringing, his confusion over his son's taste for fast food was heart wrenching. He had walked many miles during a famine when he was that age. I was a teenager in 1970s suburban America where physical labor might consist of riding my bicycle to meet friends at the community pool. And we always had enough money for a candy bar or ice cream. As an adult I came to appreciate my own father's Great Depression tales of scavenging for scrap metal in order to make enough money to go to the movies. Still, the challenges of life in other countries were more extreme.

That semester's class performances were markedly better than usual, and I credit the mix of students for that.

"A class is like a herd of cattle," one of my graduate school professors once remarked. I was a bit offended, but more amused, chalking it up to fact that this was a course in The American Frontier, and he was trying to get us to understand herd behavior. Once a professor, it did not take long for me to see what he meant. Students' behaviors – liveliness, enthusiasm, apathy, misery – tend to feed off one another's. In each class, each semester, this new group of people would behave as a group, based on some invisible force, some instinctual and silent communication. This class was among my best, and it had everything to do with the students enrolled. Heleine's presence added an extra dimension, for to be learning alongside someone who had come from Haiti made history more real and tangible.

That was also the time in which I met Renate. Someone from the Heartland Center let me know about her work in Haiti, and that she was back in the Chicago area for a visit. At that point she was working as a co-director of the University of Fondwa. Her story seemed an interesting one and certainly worthy of a presentation to my class. I gave her directions to my room and looked forward to meeting her. The first time I saw her, I felt a sense of warmth and familiarity difficult to describe. She is small and dynamic and I immediately sensed her calm and fearlessness in dealing with whatever it was that life had put before her. I felt immediately at ease. I described my comfort with her as an unarticulated common bond among those who understood social justice and humanitarian work, wherever in the world. That must have sounded so absurd to her, as it was a terribly pretentious way of putting it.

I recognized my awkwardness in these matters and inability to find the right words during a discussion with a student some years before. We had led efforts to collect donations for victims of Hurricane Mitch in Honduras. When he told me of his remarkable past work in relief efforts, I was very impressed.

"You must feel good about that," I said to him. He looked at me, surprised that I would make such a comment.

"No," he replied. He was a devout Christian who exuded pure humility in every way. "It's just what we do." And then he went on to cite Scripture to illustrate why he said what he said, and what I said sounded all the more wrong. It was as if I had accused him of being arrogant. He seemed almost ashamed that he had told me of his good deeds at all, and in that moment I learned something precious about pride and self-righteousness.

When I struggled to find meaning in my comfort with Renate in our first meeting, perhaps it was in contrast to my discomfort with others who saw me as chasing rainbows and my words just came out poorly. Some might explain the feeling of familiarity I sensed with her as a sign that we had spent a past life together. And perhaps there was a time when I would have explained it in that way, too. But I have come to learn through experience that such first feelings can indicate future work together. At that time I had no plans to work with Renate, or even see her again. But we did become reconnected.

Her presentation to the class about the University of Fondwa did just what I had hoped it would. It helped students connect more closely with Haiti. They were also able to learn something about college life under very different circumstances and were exposed a bit more to the idea that human action can change history. The work being done at the University of Fondwa had a purpose; it was inspired, intentional, and strategic and it responded to dire needs.

Fondwa is situated south of Port-au-Prince, just far enough to be rural. Life there flows with the rhythm of country life and seemed a perfect setting for the development of unique post-secondary programs. Starting with a handful of students, Renate and her co-workers established programs in management and agronomy, designed in ways that would employ graduates meaningfully in their home villages once they were finished with their studies. Productive and sustainable agriculture continued to be of primary importance to Haiti's future and providing the knowledge and skills necessary for long term growth could help students make a difference. The majority of Haiti's post-secondary agronomy programs were still centered in Port-au-Prince, and as many as 80 percent of the country's trained agronomists held office jobs there. The mission of the University of Fondwa was to bring students from rural areas and send them back to apply what they learned where it was most needed. The fact that a small group of people could take it upon themselves to create such a school was awe inspiring.

In addition to the class presentation, I scheduled a campus-wide one that evening, which was open to the community. The turnout was wonderful. Thinking back, perhaps Renate was hoping to inspire some donations and I don't know whether she did. I do know, however, that her message was well-received. Some prominent people were there and the feedback was encouraging. Some of the students in my class appeared to hear her once again. That was good to see. Very importantly, I wanted them to see the strength of human action. Empowering students to take on leadership roles can be challenging.

The study of history can sometimes be seen as abstract and irrelevant. Perhaps that is due to the way in which it is taught or perhaps those to whom it is being taught are not quite prepared to hear the whole story, to receive the message in its entirety. History is the account, or many accounts, of achievement and change. If people of the past had stood still and done nothing, there would be no such thing as history. For better or worse, it is indeed the course of human action. Renate's talk came at the right time in the semester, as students had become well-acquainted with the struggles Haitians had faced and the many attempts to make improvements. The talk also came to the right students. They got it. Each had been active on campus, and would continue to be active in their post-graduation lives. And by active, I mean taking action. Appropriate action to make a positive difference for the future.

The University of Fondwa made a difference in people's lives, and we will never know just how far the ripples begun by this educational endeavor would reach. Perhaps it could have done more. We will not know that, either. The buildings of the campus were destroyed in the earthquake, and they could no longer take any students.

18
ASSIGNED READINGS

Carefully assigning travel literature and commentaries from decades gone by can improve students' chances of understanding Haiti's difficult history and contemporaries' interpretations of it. John Dryden Kuser's *Haiti: Its Dawn of Progress after Years in a Night of Revolution* is one possibility. It tells the story of "salvation" by American troops who occupied the country during the early part of the 20th century. In 1921 he wrote: "Haitian agitators, supported by ill-advised Americans, have spread propaganda favoring the withdrawal of the United States from Haiti. Included in the propaganda have been the absurd accusations against the marines of cruelty toward the natives." He went on to say, "The question of any cruelty or unnecessary killings has been conclusively disproven by the findings of a Court of Inquiry sent to Haiti, and which has recently published its findings. As to the withdrawal of the United States from Haiti – such a course would be a menace to the world and a sad neglect of duty by the United States."

It is not easy for some students to grasp the depth of these statements when they have not yet been properly introduced to the history of U.S. foreign policy in Latin America and elsewhere. The attacks on and occupation of countries in Central America and the Caribbean have been frequent. During the early decades of the 20th century alone, the United States military occupied not only Haiti, but also Nicaragua, the Dominican Republic, a portion of Mexico's Gulf region, and Cuba from time to time. When the U.S. threatened its attack on Iraq in 2003, an organization called Historians against the War was given birth. It was no coincidence that a notable percentage of its members taught Latin American history. Latin Americanists are very familiar with past episodes there, which often parallel U.S. actions in other parts of the world. As was the case with Kuser's work, atrocities abroad went largely ignored or were rationalized in the name of doing good for those who needed our help.

There is no doubt that studying U.S. intervention in Haiti shaped my perspectives on the U.S. war in Iraq. At the same time, the war in Iraq influenced ways in which I taught history. Again, presentism was at play. Once the unrestrained patriotism of the very early 2000s subsided and the purpose and execution of the war were being challenged, students had grown ready for a bigger dose of U.S. foreign policy history so they could better contextualize events unfolding in their own lives. I envied the courage of other faculty in Historians against the War who were far more activist in their teaching. There were times in my own past when I had been more bold, but at the onset of the war I had hungry mouths to feed and did not yet have tenure. As the attack neared, a few students became increasingly agitated and wanted to talk about the situation in class. Following their lead, I devoted an entire world history class period in early March of 2003 to letting them vent and debate. As a result, I was reprimanded by the department chair, as such a discussion apparently had no place in world history.

Teaching Caribbean History during the fall 2008

semester I was feeling a bit more daring. With tenure under my belt and years of developing the course, it was time to change up my reading assignments significantly. One of the books I decided to use was Mary A. Renda's *Taking Haiti: Military Occupation and the Culture of U.S. Imperialism, 1915-1940*. It was a well-respected work illustrating paternalism and the ways in which it influenced U.S. behavior in Haiti before and throughout occupation. U.S. policy makers and those who executed strategies often viewed the objects of their help as childlike and incapable of taking care of themselves. In the early decades of the 20th century this was grounded in race theory, which classified people of the world in ways that justified U.S. and European presence in Latin America, Africa, and Asia.

The notion of U.S. paternalism is grasped more easily by some college students. The ones more apt to acknowledge it have paid closer attention to alternative news sources addressing current events or are actively uncovering truths about the American past that they had not been taught in high school. For students whose own cultural past has been underrepresented in history books, shedding new light on issues of race, ethnicity and gender give them a sense that their story is finally being told. This is certainly true of students on my campus, which is among the most diverse of the Baccalaureate/Master's institutions in Indiana. Indiana may not seem diverse, but in our corner of the state, multiple backgrounds abound. Ours is Lake County, bordering Chicago and Lake Michigan and reaching south into vast cornfields. It is snubbed by both Illinoisans and the remainder of Hoosiers, lying in some netherworld. Students reared in white suburban sprawl, Latinos from an all but post-industrial East Chicago, and blacks from a struggling Gary often occupy one room for the first time in their lives when they come to us. Often they are the first in their families to seek a university degree. They generally come expecting to hear the history they have been taught before and are surprised to learn about revolutionary women, Chicano politics, island slavery, and labor leaders – at least from a few of us. Sometimes they squirm, and sometimes they come alive.

It is a shame that such subjects or approaches are considered inappropriate by conservatives or those who wish to avoid controversy at all costs. What I like to do best is be guided by students. I can see when I have struck a chord in them, and happily follow with more information and sources. Students are good at leading the way if you give them permission and the tools to do so. This approach is not all that rare; at least I hope it is not. Nor are the kinds of students we have. Once while attending a meeting of the North Central Conference of Latin Americanists held at St. Norbert College in DePere, Wisconsin, a young graduate student confronted a professor on a panel who had just presented his work on foreign-initiated housing development in southern Mexico. The group was representative of those who taught Latin American Studies primarily in Wisconsin, Iowa, and Minnesota, and bordering states in the Upper Midwest. The professor was of the 60s generation, avowedly liberal, and proud of his work in the Peace Corps and more recently with Habitat for Humanity.

"Isn't that just like the 'White Man's Burden'?" the student asked him point blank. He referred to the legacy articulated in Rudyard Kipling's 1899 poem warning the United States of the difficult responsibility that lay ahead following the close of the Spanish-American War. As a result of the 1898 conflict, the United States gained possession – to one degree or another – of Cuba, Puerto Rico, Guam, and the Philippines. In the same year but in a different maneuver it also took the Hawaiian Islands. For many, that time marked the beginning of U.S. imperialism, if one ignores its expansionistic conquest of Native American nations through the 19th century. It also provided evidence of racist influences in foreign policy.

"Excuse me?" the professor asked the student. The young man swallowed hard, overcame any hesitation, and spoke with passion. Students sometimes attend these types of regional academic conferences, but rarely speak. His own brownness stood out at this mostly white – however altruistic – Catholic school not far from Green Bay. He had come to Wisconsin from New Mexico.

"Don't you think that Habitat for Humanity workers are arrogant in the way that they go into other countries and build houses with their own kind of style, imposing them on the people there? White attitudes have not changed over the past century. These people are perfectly willing to build their own kind of housing if they just have the means to do it." It was a genuinely awkward moment, painful for the professor and a bit enlightening for me, as I had never looked at the work of Habitat for Humanity in that way. He was speaking not only from a different ethno-cultural perspective, but as a member of a new generation.

It has become almost a rite of passage for some liberal arts and social science majors on many campuses to embrace the kind of work Renda puts forth as a way of validating their newfound perspectives. Not so with this class in 2008. It is true that every class is different. This time there was a preacher enrolled, and he was rather charismatic. He was probably in his 50s – more than twice the age of the other students – and led a congregation at a small, nearby church. He spoke eloquently and often, and even when they seemed to disagree with him, he commanded their respect. They did not argue with him. After all, he was a preacher.

He and I did not vie for the favor of the group. At least I do not think we did. I sensed his disagreement with my positions and another faculty member might have wrestled more for control of the classroom. Perhaps I would have tried to at an earlier point in my career. But I did not see it as an issue of control so much as an opportunity to remind students to make their best attempts to distinguish fact from opinion, and demonstrate respect for conflicting perspectives. I knew which of his statements were fact and which were opinion, and the situation forced me to become more sensitive to which of mine were which.

He had traveled extensively on mission trips and his insight was valuable to the other students. I gave him an opportunity to share photos with the class and cringed at some of his descriptions of how much people in Latin America needed us. Especially disturbing were pictures of him and associates posing with paramilitaries in Colombia. It had been some time since I read of armed forces aligning with missionaries in counterinsurgency efforts, and I did not feel at all prepared to raise the issue in a way that might confront his intentions or his work there. Rather, I encouraged the class to read more on the subject when they had a chance.

When it came time to discuss the Renda book this student artfully dismissed it. Members of the class had read it to varying degrees, as was the case with most assigned readings. But he seemed to have read, and was prepared to argue, every word. No matter what Renda said, how she said it, or what sources she used to provide evidence of her argument, he did not see paternalism as a factor in the U.S. occupation of Haiti. Given his experiences, he probably did not want to see it. What made me most uneasy was his attempt to wrangle other students into discrediting the book as well. Maybe that was my perception. Perhaps the experiences they brought to class had laid a foundation for rejecting her work, as well. When I brought up the value of noting credentials in addition to evidence when legitimizing a position a student sitting near him turned to a blurb on the book cover.

"Assistant Professor of history and women's studies at Mount Holyoke," he read of Renda's title.

"Ahh… that explains it," said another. They made wisecracks about women's studies in the back of the room. Renda's work in women's studies may have influenced her view of paternalism and/or vice versa, but I could not believe there still seemed a need to defend the discipline in the 2000s.

Years before, I might have more readily challenged their resistance to acknowledging U.S. paternalism in foreign policy, or more enthusiastically encouraged them to see it as a possibility based on the sources at hand. Later in my career some thoughtful pearls of wisdom might have tripped more easily off my tongue. But at this point, I found little to say. I stood there with a greater consciousness of disparate human angles, wondering if anything I said could influence them. Self-doubts in teaching are common and this was one of those moments when I questioned my impact. Years into the profession we find ourselves wondering if students are ever going to stop making the same mistakes, but then we step back and realize that they are not the same students who came to us ten years, or even one year, before. They are not necessarily making the same mistakes. Yes, we are repeating ourselves, but to a new group of students who have not yet heard what we have to say.

Accepting the history of U.S. paternalism in Haiti, however, is not the same as having students improve their paragraph development on essay exams or seeing them finally distinguish between there, their, and they're. And I would not want a roomful of students who easily accepted that there was such a thing, just because I said so or because they had read one book on the subject. Perhaps this was simply their first taste of it and they would come to see it later on. Perhaps they would see future foreign policy developments through a different lens because they had had this discussion. What I saw most of all, however, was a clash of world views. The preacher and I had similar years of experience on the planet and in traveling abroad. But we had come to this point, in the classroom, having developed strikingly different interpretations. He had nothing but good intentions in what he saw his life's work to be, and nor did I.

19
CHRISTINE

During the fall semester of 2009, I made preparations for my trip to meet with Renate in Jeremie and then Port-au-Prince. During the previous couple years I had served as Director of International Programs, a position that allowed me a seemingly unlimited travel budget for purposes of professional development. My return to faculty status, compounded with university budget slashing driven by the failing economy, brought my travel allotment down to about $500 per year. A severe cut in my salary loomed and I wondered how I was going to find money for this trip. I had recently taken out a home equity loan to remodel my kitchen and bathroom and I underestimated the expenses I would incur in raising three kids. I was not sure if my new take home pay would cover the bills. First world worries to be sure. Real for me, nonetheless.

As is the case from time to time, I wondered aloud as I walked into one of my classes. Having just had a conversation with a colleague about how I might justify the value of such a trip both for research and faculty development, I moaned to my class about the financial frustrations of being a professor.

"What do they expect me to do?" I muttered as I placed my books on the desk. I was feeling very much like a single parent unable to afford the extra investment in opportunities that would make my work more satisfying and job promotion more likely. Faculty outside the humanities and social sciences generally take home significantly larger paychecks, and for the many who were married and had a double income, frequent travel was a given. Once in Haiti, my expenses would run several hundred dollars even with the most meager of accommodations, and the airfare to Miami, Port-au-Prince, Jeremie and back was another $800 or so.

The class to which I griped that day was Modern Latin American History, comprised mainly of upper-level students. They knew of my plans, and understood how much this trip meant to the quality of my work – undoubtedly less so to the quality of my sanity. Though I did not want to discourage any of them from the vocation of an academic life, I confessed periodically a bit about what, exactly, that was – many years of schooling, unfunded research, countless hurdles, egos and nonsense, along with all its rewards. Most of them are first generation college students, and have not had role models to watch meander their ways through the process. Each time I successfully presented a conference paper or had an article published I shared the experience with them. I was a first generation college student, as well, except for the few accounting classes my father took at a local school. Finding my way through the maze of higher learning without a mentor was difficult, and I knew that casual mentions of what I was going through would clue them in a bit.

I went on with my lecture, and that was that. I felt committed to the trip and knew the money situation would work itself out. It always did. Haiti was where I need to be to get grounded again and put any challenges I thought I had into better perspective.

Following the next class meeting, one of my students approached me in the hall.

"Professor—" I turned to see that it was Christine. She had done extraordinarily well in a number of my classes and was one of my more unique students.

The first time I met her was in a 100-level U.S. history survey. She sat in the front row and I could not help but notice her. She was around my age, had striking blond hair, magazine cover quality makeup, fantastic shoes, and a full-length fur coat. Thick. I will be the first to admit I know little about fur, but I do know it was not rabbit. Her perfume was subtle and expensive. I wondered what the other students thought of her.

She turned out to be a perfect scholar. Smart. Very. Hardworking. Reliable. Our occasional conversations became increasingly frequent, and we came to learn her daughters were about the same ages as my sons and attended the same high school. Her natural curiosity about history was outstanding, and as mothers of teenagers we developed an additional bond. She eventually dressed like the other students – plus perfect hair and makeup – and seemed to make some very good friends.

"Professor, may I talk with you about your trip to Haiti?"

"Sure." I wondered what she had in mind. Occasionally students and colleagues kick around the idea of joining me on a trip and, to be honest, I wondered how she could be serious. As down to earth as I came to know her to be, I did not think she could survive the rigors of life in Haiti.

"What's up?"

"I know this might sound crazy . . ."

"Yes?"

"... and please let me know if I'm being too forward in any way." She took a breath. "It's just that I am so impressed with your travels, and my husband and I were talking... Well, we had to go to this thing last night. A $300-a-plate thing. I do get so tired of them. Making small talk, and wondering if this or that is making any kind of difference."

"So?"

"So, I told my husband about your trip and asked if we might be able to fund it. At least part of it."

"What?" My jaw dropped. Yes, it was awkward, though not enough to keep me from agreeing.

"I don't know what to say."

"Don't say anything. Just let us do it. Please. This will help students there, right?"

"I hope so. I just don't kn—"

"So it's settled. I'll have my husband cut the check this afternoon."

The following week she brought me a check for $800, written from her husband's business, a local construction firm known in the area for its lucrative contracts. I was so grateful. Embarrassed that I had fretted about the poor economic status of college faculty, I secretly promised to someday direct my gratitude monetarily in some way to Haitians. This trip would just be a stepping stone.

"There is just one thing we ask in return."

"Ok." I wondered what she had in mind.

"We would like it so much if you could make a presentation about your trip for our friends when you return."

"Of course! Of course, I will!" That was easy. Professors are used to going on about one thing or another at the drop of a hat. "That's not a problem at all."

"Good. Oh, thank you so much. Not to raise money or anything. Just for information. I'll book a room at the country club. Innsbrook."

"No, thank you. Really." Country club? It sounded a bit surreal. But I looked forward to visiting Innsbrook. I had never been there.

The gift was a godsend. I don't know what I would have done without it.

20
LOST LUGGAGE

I had never experienced lost luggage until this trip and as much as I desired to commiserate with friends I hesitated to mention it lest they equate it with Haitian dysfunction and magnify negative perceptions they might have had of the country. It was not Haiti's fault.

The morning I left Chicago, temperatures had plummeted into the single digits, and icing on the plane had caused some malfunction. When American Airlines opted to take the aircraft out of commission and put me on a later flight, I assured myself it was for the best. However, I had already checked my luggage.

Never having lost luggage before, I had become confident, perhaps too much so, and neglected to prepare for such a situation. Rather than pack necessities, an extra change of clothing, etc., in my carry-on, I checked nearly everything. Knowing I would be leaving a frigid climate for a much warmer one and going through the process of changing planes in Miami, I wanted to be free to travel light. I carried only my stylish red briefcase, normally reserved for my laptop, and put in it only a book of crossword puzzles, a legal pad, some pens, a couple of Luna Bars, a book called *Courageous Dreaming*, and a copy of Graham Green's *The Comedians*, given to me by my cousin. He traveled and read a good deal and knew a lot of good books about Americans in foreign countries. Renate and I hoped to have lunch at the Hotel Oloffson one day and I wanted so much to finish it before then. I was sure it would give me a whole new outlook on the setting. Reading it in the airport would help in the mental and cultural transitions between Chicago and Port-au-Prince, at least that is what I had hoped. The last place I remember seeing it was lying on a bench at O'Hare.

I had gotten up repeatedly to check on my flight, and the romanticism of literary accounts evidently took a back seat to my worries about the practical matters of travel. Plus there was something about this trip making me uneasy in the first place. In the days before Christmas, just more than a week before, I had spent much time shopping for a digital camera. With little in my budget, I decided on a Polaroid I saw in Target's weekly ad. I had promised Christine that I would have photos on hand for the presentation. After picking up a few other things for the trip, I found the camera, and stood waiting for what seemed an eternity at the counter. I looked at it several times as the clerk finally appeared and then waited on other customers, answering what seemed to me to be ridiculous questions.

I was not sure why I was losing my patience. I looked at the camera again, touching its red metallic body, wondering why the universe was standing in the way of what should be a simple purchase. Could I really not afford it? Should I borrow a camera from a friend? It seemed more than that. Having developed a passion for photography during college, I came to know the magic of capturing images and preserving them indefinitely into the future, after their subjects had been long gone. I peered into the lens, imagining I could see into the body of the camera, and wondered what it might hold one day.

I backed off. There was something about having that camera that scared me.

"Can I help you?" The sound of the clerk's voice startled me.

"Uh… " I had to make a decision and had to know I was not crazy. "I'm interested in this one."

"Do you have any questions?" He watched me staring at it.

"No. No, I'll take it." When I got it home, I read the short-cut instructions, charged the battery, and placed it away in my suitcase.

The night before the trip, I stayed up very late, packing everything possible in that suitcase, including my laptop, vitamins, recently prescribed thyroid medication, dried fruit and nuts, mosquito repellant, battery-operated alarm clock, flashlight, and lots of professional, conservative, yet lightweight clothing. Nerves kept me from becoming tired and I ultimately had to force myself to get a few hours' sleep. When my departure was delayed, American Airlines employees assured me I could retrieve my luggage in Port-au-Prince. The airport seemed unusually quiet, and I became lost in my thoughts about Haiti. I looked back on the holiday time with my family and wished that I had not been so preoccupied with the trip.

Once I arrived in Port-au-Prince, the warm air was refreshing, and I took as many deep breaths as I could, unconvinced that January could be like this all the time. I realized that the comfortable brown slacks, with enough polyester to give me coach seating comfort and warmth, would have to go. I could not wait to change. I took off my trench coat and tied it around my waist, and searched for my luggage. I waited and waited, but it was nowhere to be found. I took off one more layer, a cotton cardigan sweater, as my long-sleeved t-shirt was more than enough. People rushed around, to the side, in front, and behind me, all seeming to know what they were doing. That is usually the way it is in a strange airport, especially when I don't know the language. Hearing Creole all around somehow makes one feel inadequate in the most simple of functions in an airport.

I found the American Airlines counter to ease my mind. I knew there was a driver waiting for me and I did not want to delay. The woman stationed there wore a uniform similar – if not identical – to those worn at O'Hare, but her demeanor was very different. Kind, yes, but far more laid back than in the States. I have found this to be true of nearly all airline representatives in the Caribbean. It is not as if they aren't doing their jobs, it is just that they do them in such a non-U.S. sort of way. It is a difference in attitude – toward life, work, and world. She told me my luggage should be there. I was not convinced, most likely because I did not see it.

I explained that I was in Port-au-Prince for only one night, and then would be off to Jeremie on Tortug'Air. She said that my luggage would be forwarded there, but again, I was not convinced. She did not seem to have a way of tracking anything by computer. I was very pleased that American was employing Haitians in their own country, but wished very much that the company had provided them with the means to do their jobs well.

I took another deep breath, this one not to immerse myself in the Caribbean air, but to relax and feed a sense of trust that my suitcase would find its way to Jeremie. I walked carefully and with purpose past numerous men who eagerly tried to get me a taxi.

"*Non, merci,*" I said repeatedly, happy that some French

danced from my lips, but having little idea whether there was much true communication taking place. After a bit of searching I found my driver. He held a sign with my name, and we smiled at one another. He spoke next to no English, and I spoke zero Creole. But he took me to where I needed to be.

When we arrived at Hospice St. Joseph, it was not exactly how I pictured from Renate's description, but then again I was not sure what to expect. It housed a clinic on the first floor with rooms for sleeping above. It was gated, as most hotels and such are in Port-au-Prince. Much of it was painted a deep green blue and it seemed inviting. When I enter a new place and there is no reference point, no comparable past experience, no way of communicating verbally, I have learned to trust my gut to get a sense of things. My body was telling me this was a good place. I tried to explain the suitcase situation to my driver, but it was no use. I would figure that out later, I thought. We smiled at each other and I gave him a couple of dollars, knowing that the true expenses were being calculated elsewhere, and found my way through the clinic. Mothers sat with their children in chairs along the wall. It seemed both indoors and out, similar to many accommodations in warmer parts of the world. Again I smiled and again and again, and I was taken to my room. It was perfect.

It is funny how when one travels that bedding can so much define a stay. For me, whatever bedding is there makes my stay a good one, if only because it is unique and there for me when I end a long day of being out and about. I once stayed at a bed and breakfast in Lismore, Ireland, near where my grandfather was born. The room was lush and pristine, the bed graced in white cotton bedding trimmed with lace and sheets dotted with small blue flowers. The owner, almost a caricature of Irish lilt and warm, humorous story-telling, said she made annual trips to Boston to visit family and purchase the best bedding the city had to offer. It showed. I once stayed at a Victorian inn in Grand Haven, Michigan with a room so warm and inviting (it was during a brisk spring break weekend in March) that it inspired me to purchase all new bedding for my own room upon returning home. I liked the feeling of lying high on a pile of down, and wondered why I might not live like that every day. This room at Hospice St. Joseph was nothing like those. It was so simple in comparison, but perhaps the most inviting room I had ever had.

After climbing the stairs past the patients, gift shop, and dining room, I was taken through the common area of the third floor onto a small balcony, and to my room. With my back to the door, I had an amazing view of the city – hills to the left and to the right, and cement block houses taking up every square foot. Palm trees here and there reminded me just how far I had traveled from Indiana.

The room was furnished with two twin beds and a small table with a pitcher of water and two glasses. Directly across from the window was a small bathroom with a sink, shower and toilet. The tile and fixtures were far from new, but they served their purposes. The bedspreads were thin, but the weather was warm. And it was apparent special care was given to make sure they looked their best. A towel, wash cloth, and small bar of soap sat on the end of each bed. The colors of everything were bright and reminded me of my childhood.

I turned to the manager who had shown me to my room, and explained that I was missing my luggage. She graciously offered to provide a toothbrush and toothpaste. I felt terrible having to ask for anything more than was normally expected in this country of so little. But she smiled and quickly returned with them.

I poured myself a glass of water and went into the bathroom to wash my hands. I looked forward to a rest on the bed as the afternoon sun began to set. My sleep that night was more restful than I had experienced in a very long time. I liked being there. However, I was there for just one night on this part of the trip. In the morning, I would be off to Jeremie.

21
JEREMIE

I was becoming accustomed to riding in small aircraft and looked forward to my flight from Port-au-Prince's regional airport to Jeremie. The airport itself seemed a bit chaotic and again I attributed that to my lack of understanding of Creole. I tried to get some assurance that my suitcase was somehow making it from one city to another, and was told that it was most likely already there. I was beginning to feel as if some newly emerging obsessive compulsive disorder was here to plague me and tried to relax. They were only things, I thought, and reminded myself that I was in a country of so few things.

I took a seat and waited for someone to announce my flight, knowing it could well leave anywhere from 45 minutes to two hours after its scheduled departure. I looked around, watching people, as I am apt to do in any airport. And I reminisced about my sitting there with the church ladies, Tom, John, and the bishop several years before, anticipating our trip to Cap-Haïtien and then Fort Liberté.

It was different traveling alone and I had to have faith that I would make it through the process and that Renate would be at the airport in Jeremie to greet me. I did make it through the process, and yes, Renate was there to greet me. When traveling by myself in strange places for uncommon reasons, belief in a higher power seems to kick into high gear. The down time allows me to be alone in my thoughts, comparing whatever journey I am on to that of life. The progression of being taken from one place to another, from one experience to another, is just as it should be. We go where we are meant to go and are where we are meant to be. Yes, decisions and free will play significant roles, but once the trip is underway, it is best to go along, trust all will work out, and not anticipate what lies ahead with too much hope or fear. Neutral anticipation while looking around in the present is all that needs to be.

Perhaps it is my trust in a greater force – a higher energy – that allows me to travel alone under such circumstances in the first place, for I never feel alone. Call it a crutch. Call it imaginary fantasy. Call it what you will. But for me it is what it is, even if my understanding of what it is shifts continually. I looked around at the people in the airport, and wondered what they were up to and where they were headed.

Flying into the Department of the Grand'Anse, I noticed abundant vegetation that strikingly distinguished it from the barren and eroding north. We landed softly on a field of grass and I looked around to see innumerable United Nations vehicles. The area was indeed remote, and noticeably quiet, and the airport structure itself no larger than a small house. I wondered what made the U.N. presence necessary.

"Hello, hello, Kathy!" Renate greeted me with a smile and hug like no other can.

"Renate! I can't believe I'm here!"

"It is so good to see you!" I knew at that moment my decision to come was the right one. She bought some oranges and avocados from some women standing in the sunshine at a fruit stand. I loved January in the Caribbean. "Don't you have a suitcase?"

"It's lost," I told her. "My flight from Chicago to Miami was changed and I'm not sure where my bag is.

"Well, let's look here." It took all of a minute or two to scour the Jeremie airport. "No worries. We'll find it." She promised to take me to the Tortug'Air office in town the following day. A friend of hers worked there.

"Thanks I'm sure it will turn up." I was already warm and looked forward to putting on a linen shirt. "Just a quick question... "

"Sure, what is it?" she asked.

"What is the U.N. doing here?"

"They're everywhere in Haiti." She laughed. "You'll see." It was true. All along the road to the house where we were staying there were cars, SUVs, motorbikes, and trucks, all white with a large, black "U.N." emblazoned on each.

"I don't sense any tension here," I told her.

"Of course, not. There is no tension here. Haiti is a perfect place for them to be. They're from all over; mostly from Indonesia, I think."

"It is beautiful here."

"And peaceful."

"Do you think that's because the U.N. is here?"

"No." She shook her head. Even Port-au-Prince felt different to me this time. It seemed Haiti was making progress.

A local doctor was kind enough to let us stay at her house for the days we spent in Jeremie. She was from the States but now spent the majority of her time in Haiti, returning only occasionally to make enough money to live on the remainder of the year. She was away in Milwaukee giving full use of her home to Renate and me. Also staying with us for the next few days was Corinne, a psychology professor who was a friend of Renate.

The house was situated perhaps one hundred feet from the road and surrounded by trees. Each time we drove in I noticed a woman and her children nearby. They were very friendly and Renate spoke to them in Creole about any number of things. The houses were spaced not too far apart, and I wondered which one was theirs and how they became such close neighbors. Then I noticed the woman sweeping the steps. And her son, who must have been nine or ten-years-old was there to help us every time we appeared. He retrieved gasoline for the generator and for the truck, and seemed to eagerly await Renate's suggestions of what to do next.

"Where do they live?" I asked her.

"On the porch," she replied. "Didn't I tell you?"

Haitian society is still comprised largely of an informal economy and informal housing. People will do what they can to make a few *gourdes* to feed themselves and their families. And the money I saw the boy earn from Renate seemed to mean everything to him. I had never seen anyone so eager to work. I hoped that one day he would have an opportunity to go far. He certainly had the desire.

One afternoon the daughter ran up to Renate, waving a sheet of paper. Renate looked at it and smiled, saying something that seemed to please her.

"She did very well on her report card. She wanted to show it to us."

"Nice," I said, impressed that she could concentrate so hard in school when living on a porch with her mother and siblings.

"Academic achievement is such a priority here. It is amazing."

I agreed. The look on her face was inspiring, and wondered if I had commended my own children enough on their accomplishments when they were young. Their father and I were both teachers so we expected them to do their best in school, but I doubted they knew how much we really cared. Later, we saw the girl walking with her friends along the road. She beamed, knowing that we knew that she was a good student.

The first floor of the doctor's house was the only original part of the structure. It had three bedrooms, two bathrooms, and a kitchen. The ceiling was low and the hallways a bit uneven and winding, but it provided what we needed and more. These were very good conditions in Haiti. Being there makes one much more aware of our own habits of consumption. Fueling a generator to run a refrigerator seems excessive, so it becomes more sensible to buy a few simple foods – some vegetables, fruits, a few eggs, butter, and bread – and consume them before they can go bad. The benefits of eating vegetarian are more apparent, as meat production is very costly and takes a tremendous toll on the planet when comparable nutrition can be found much more simply in plant products. Grinding coffee beans is a way of life – good coffee is expected everywhere in the Caribbean and lighting the stove each time to heat the percolator makes one more appreciative of every cup. The door was rarely closed during the day and chickens wandered in and out while we cooked and sat down at the table to eat.

The doctor had raised money to add on to the house building an impressive second and third floor above. Their ceilings were a good deal higher, and the concrete walls heavy. It was a wonder the lower level could sustain them. There were multiple rooms whose walls and floors were still raw and dusty where medical students from abroad would one day be able to stay, and gather for meetings. The accommodations were designed to be very valuable for those coming to do clinical work in the area. The residents of the area were in need of any medical care that was offered.

Though the first floor was dark and lit only sporadically in the evening when we decided the effort was worth it, the upper floors were bright and breezy. Large window openings captured hours of daylight more readily available above the tree tops. From the third floor balcony there was a beautiful and clear view of the sea in the distance. I hoped the future student visitors could appreciate just how lucky they were to be housed in such a place.

My room downstairs was furnished with a twin bed and small table, and the window invited fresh, warm air and sounds of country animals all hours of the day and night.

22
MENTAL HEALTH

Renate and Corinne were very busy in their psychology research and it was interesting to watch them exchange ideas. The work of the historian takes place primarily in solitude. We sometimes converse in ways that further our efforts, but mostly our communication is conducted with dead people who have left behind records, hints of what they were thinking, and evidence of what they accomplished in their lives on earth. It is our job to interpret what happened and how it influenced other events or human actions.

Some claim the discipline is a social science, while others consider it part of the humanities. I tend to fall into the latter category. It is not purely literature in that it is not imagined. And while we work with evidence grounded in real time and place, our methods are not scientific, not in an empirical sense. I was happy to have the opportunity to see two experts in psychology at work. They contemplated studies related to living human beings and deliberated how to apply what they knew in the community. More so, they were investigating ways to see the people of the Grand'Anse address their own issues.

Renate first came to Haiti several years before to perform sleep research. Looking for a society more reliant on the patterns of the sun than the artificially lit Chicago, she fell in love with Haiti and its people. She decided to spend as much time there as her funding would allow, and continued work at the University of Chicago essentially to support her ventures when grant money was no longer available. I am not sure what initially drew Corinne there, but she eventually married a Haitian man, had a child, and held a strong commitment to Haitian development. She and I talked some about her field, and she told me she was very pleased to be teaching in one of the few humanist psychology departments in the United States at the University of West Georgia.

They were working together to create a mental health clinic in Jeremie. At this point they were engaged in data collection through surveys to see what kinds of services were needed. They were also brainstorming possible ways in which they could match their work to existing Haitian concepts in order to see the dialogue unfold more freely. Even though the community was embracing the idea of a mental health clinic, this would be the first of its kind. The vocabulary of mental health did not yet exist. When I asked how they might go about teaching the vocabulary, Corinne pointed out that it was not so much teaching, as it was attempting to foster a culture where concepts of mental health challenges might be recognized. Until that happened there could be no real vocabulary, for what are words but symbols for concepts? The need for mental health practitioners in the Grand'Anse was great.

Finding cross-cultural parallels for ideas had posed challenges. In working with a local teacher, Corinne saw an opportunity to see whether a survey might be done conducted his school, giving her a chance to find out what kinds of issues exist among the children. A standard survey might prove difficult as they were still deciding what the questions might be. Rather, she considered that teachers might be asked open-ended questions, requesting that they note their observations of any particularly unusual behavior exhibited by a student in the classroom. It seemed a good starting place. At that point they were engaged in simple brainstorming, which in my experience has proved integral to good projects. It was interesting to observe how others utilize it in work about which I knew nothing.

In following days, I would get to learn much more. Renate and Corinne prepared a presentation for local students and health care providers to be held at the Université de la Nouvelle Grand'Anse, locally referred to as UNOGA. It was a small technical school located about five kilometers outside Jeremie, which offered programs in management an agronomy. The grounds were lush green with plots for farming demonstrations, pig husbandry, and chicken coops. There were two classroom buildings, offices, and a large assembly hall spread far apart with areas of grass in between. The overcast sky and the humid air made the campus warm and inviting, while still feeling spacious.

In the large, marble-tiled room of the administration building, Renate and Corinne set up their laptop and projector as twenty or so people from the community arrived and took their seats. I was honored to be their slide changer. They spoke to the group in Creole, and I was able to understand the gist of what they were conveying through the magic of PowerPoint. I also watched body language carefully to see evidence of communication and understanding. It is surprising how much we can rely on alternative methods of understanding when challenged to do so. They spoke of signs and symptoms of stress, a topic familiar to me. The timing was perfect, for what they said reinforced what I needed to hear.

Toward the end of their talk, they introduced a relaxation exercise through meditation. I was content to continue my role as audio-visual assistant in the back of the room, but found myself joining in as everyone closed their eyes and began deep breathing. It was something members of the audience had not done, and something I needed to do. By the time it was over, a sense of incredible calm came over the room, and then smiles emerged as people became conscious of the effects it had on them. It was beautiful. At that moment there was nowhere else on earth I would rather be.

23
Teaching

Though Renate was busy catching up on her work, she kept her promise to introduce me to teachers in the area so I could learn more about the educational system from their perspectives. Peter was one. He worked nearby and had become a good friend of both her and Corinne. I was anxious to learn from him what teachers' lives were like and what they hoped to offer their students. Renate acted as interpreter.

Peter was a secondary school teacher of experimental sciences, physics, and biology. He was 26-years-old and had been teaching for six years. This was my first interview and I was admittedly a bit apprehensive, but he welcomed any questions from me and was thoughtful and considerate in his answers. He seemed a conscientious teacher.

According to Peter, a major problem in education there was understandably a lack of resources for facilities, materials, and salaries. He described his school as neither public nor private, but more a "community" school, where funding was unpredictable. He added that finances were not much more predictable in other schools. He negotiated a salary of less than one dollar per hour at the beginning of the school year, though the director had not been able to pay him regularly. The lack of resources had made the school itself inter-pedagogical.

Whereas the blending of disciplines and age groups had been targets of innovation in wealthier school districts in the United States, they had become necessities in much of Haiti, where demands on teachers were especially high.

Peter was honest about the challenges he faced; for example, his school building was hot and benches intended to seat four students were forced to seat ten or eleven. Attendance was good, except following heavy rains. The students were eager to learn, and often walked an hour or two to school each day. Education, they felt, was the best path to a life of something better. I wondered what it must be like to teach the sciences with few materials and no laboratory facilities. He said the students in his school were fortunate to be using books, but had no opportunity to conduct experiments themselves. There were no test tubes, beakers, Bunsen burners, or whatever else might serve as basic provisions in a science classroom. I recalled my own 7th grade science class, which was home to our first real lab table. It was portable and small in comparison to what we would have later on, but it allow us chance to demonstrate experiments ourselves in front of the class. And seeing cells under a microscope for the first time made all the difference in the world. I wondered how he could convey what he needed without a hands-on experience for the students.

According to Peter, the funding for his school was consistently erratic, start-up money coming by way of special donations with some follow-up funding from time to time from the European Union or elsewhere. In recent days, political candidates had made appearances with some donations in hand, as national elections were scheduled for later that year. It was common for money to flow when politicians were campaigning, but he predicted that once the elections were over, the money would vanish.

What he told me was interesting and reinforced what I thought to be true about schooling in Haiti. As it was my first interview I was not sure yet what to ask, for I had nothing with which I could compare. In addition, having Renate interpret was a little awkward. I felt as if I had just arrived and was not quite acclimated to the area. Still, it was good. I was looking forward to talking with social studies teachers about their ideas on civics education. When the conversation took a turn, I learned just how committed Peter was in this area. He devoted much of his free time to educating people in his community about political engagement, urging them to learn about candidates and vote thoughtfully, based on what would prove beneficial for the community and not for personal gain. He said he wanted people to notice how candidates appeared with food and campaign promises before elections and how in a poor region that can be quite powerful. Peter encouraged prospective voters to think in the long term.

I asked him, with a smile, why he became a teacher. I suppose I was expecting some heartfelt response and a smile in return. Instead, he said it was not really a matter of choice. As is often the case in Haiti, a profession is chosen for you. Peter had been working in agronomy, and at some point had been asked to teach. He admitted it was difficult at first and very stressful, but he had come to find satisfaction in it. He also had initiated projects to teach community members how to create and maintain vegetable gardens. Growing one's own food can enhance nutrition exponentially. Even though he did not plan for a career in teaching, Peter seemed a natural.

Our conversation turned to agriculture. Food production gets a good deal of attention by people of various sectors in Haiti. Corinne, too, had worked in food production, I believe affiliated somehow with the Ministry of Agriculture.

She said she was often asked how a psychologist ends up in agronomy. She said she tells people that just one egg a day could ensure proper cognitive development in a Haitian child. Haitian egg production had been devastated by imports from the United States and more recently from the Dominican Republic. She described the massive truckloads of eggs coming across the Dominican border regularly.

I recalled talking with an agronomist on my 2003 visit who was then working with Catholic Relief Services. We had some candid discussions about genetically modified food. At that time there was increasing concern about GMOs among my colleagues in global education and friends involved in the Slow Food movement. But his comments were quite unexpected. First, he said that the opposition to GMOs in some circles was in fact originating from market competition between the European Union and United States that really had little to do with the developing world. When people were hungry, he reminded me, notions of long term effects on organisms were trumped by the immediate need to produce food – as much food as possible in the shortest amount of time. The example he used was egg production. If, he argued, they could introduce hens that had been engineered to lay more eggs to roam and breed among the existing poultry population, they could alter the capacity for Haitians to consume this otherwise easily produced protein. He became noticeably spirited when making his case. It looked not so much due to any political position or resentment; rather out of a genuine desire to feed people of his country quickly.

Corinne was no supporter of GMOs and I got the impression that Peter was not either. We returned to the topic of teaching science, but I could see that he envisioned the world in the long term. Teachers are conditioned to do that, for patience is everything. The fruits of one's labors often cannot be seen for a very long time.

24
Catharsis

Ventilation from the large windows in my room helped a good deal when it came time to wash my clothes. I found a couple of hangers and did my best to keep my limited wardrobe functioning, alternating what little I had.

Each of the first few days Renate and I checked with the local travel office to see if my suitcase had arrived. We had no luck. But sitting quietly in my room set the perfect stage for thinking more about possessions. I was entering a Zen stage of life in which I considered letting go of the vast majority of my things one day soon, keeping only what I needed to get by. Having been a suburban dweller all my life made it easier said than done, for this typical American lifestyle draws more things into the picture, perhaps because we have the space to hold those things. Or perhaps we create the space to hold all the things that we have. Visiting places like Haiti and observing just what it is that people need to live provides good teaching moments, or I should say learning moments. I am the eternal student there. But not having much due to lost luggage was beginning to wear on me.

I went through computer withdrawal. Internet access in the house was rare, and Corinne did let me use hers to check my e-mail. But after some time it seemed hardly worth the trouble. It required firing up the generator and then hoping there was an adequate internet connection. Having misplaced my copy of *The Comedians*, I resorted to reading *Courageous Dreaming*. In recent years I had accumulated a number of New Age self-help books on the recommendations of friends or just browsing through Barnes and Noble. I could not remember where I got this one or why I decided to bring it along, but it was the only thing I had to read. And it intrigued me.

The author, whose name I do not remember, discussed various levels of dreaming and what it took to develop the power to dream things into being, consciously and with intention. I wondered how I might do this, or how anyone might do this, but never took the time to actively put it into practice. And now, as is the case with the content of so many books from my past, I have forgotten what I read. At the time it added to my escape from the reality that had seemed to strangle me over the previous year or so. It also helped to have a legal pad and something to write with. I was perfectly content to sit on my bed and put pen to paper.

My purpose in making this trip was to take some recent experiences in education and re-envision the basics of its intentions. To some degree, I wanted to rethink academia altogether. Over the years I had been trained to see things academically, to approach the world academically, to research relentlessly, and write on the basis of my findings. For a long time I worked with books, articles, manuscripts, primary source documents, and notes, notes, and more notes. Notes on slips of paper, notes in notebooks, and notes on note cards. My notes were recreated, parroted in the text, and cited in footnotes and endnotes. The work of the historian is generated by text and in text. To those in the humanities the text is bestowed more validity than the words of live people, for people can be biased, people can be emotional, people might speak based on something other than reason, making what they say less truthful. To acknowledge this through analysis is permitted, but only through dehumanizing the writer.

Regardless of the fact that text itself is the product of human beings, once something is in writing it is given more weight, and if it is documented and re-documented and documented once more, it achieves a level of truth unmatched by any spoken work or other kind of writing. That is the stuff of academia. To reveal to any colleagues that I had even owned a book like *Courageous Dreaming* would have been sacrilege. And to write, then and there, with a pen on a legal pad which happened to be in my bag could not possibly produce anything of worth. A personal diary, perhaps, a journal to relieve tension, release creativity, to satisfy no one but myself. To spend time. To kill time. And, yet, all I could do was to write. Time felt immeasurable, and incapable of being killed.

In preparation for the trip I began to gather materials about Haiti and to write down ideas, intending to contextualize an outline for my research and give it a direction. My preliminary studies helped to provide a list of topics and subtopics to keep in mind once I was able to make observations regarding Haitian education on the ground there. I began by taking notes, and more notes, paraphrasing, analyzing, synthesizing, and there it was, the beginning of something, someday worthy of publication by a scholarly press.

But the urge to write freely would not subside. During the months before that January trip, no matter how hard I tried to stop it, I churned out page after page of my earlier experiences in Haiti, my curiosity about Haiti, and my feelings about Haiti and Haitians. Yes, feelings. I put it aside, consciously acknowledging that I must have some cathartic need to do it, to get it out of my system, and mentally categorized it as some sort of self-therapy. Then I returned to my academic research. I did what I could to find sources on the history of education in Haiti.

Once in my room in Jeremie, with nothing but a few pieces of clothing hanging in the breeze at the window, two Luna Bar wrappers, a book of half-filled crossword puzzles, and a work about dreaming new realities, I wrote. I wrote and I wrote and I wrote. Donkeys brayed and rooster crowed and children played in the yard. Renate checked on my from time to time, but I assured her I was fine. After I filled both sides of every page of my legal pad, I asked her if there was a place in town where I could buy some more paper.

"Yes, you can probably buy some at the store when we go there tomorrow," she said. And we did the next day, and I wrote some more.

Later that evening, Corinne and I spent some more time talking. Conversation in English was much appreciated. She was able to get a bit of internet service, just enough to quickly check word from home. We laughed about what we took for granted in the States. Renate was out visiting with friends and I had had enough of solitude. We looked around for something to do. It was very kind of the doctor to let us use her home while she was away, but I felt a bit uncomfortable looking through magazines and such in her room.

"I found something to watch," Corinne said. She was holding a multiple DVD set of *I Love Lucy*. We set her laptop on the dresser, pulled up two chairs, and watched episode after episode. Yes, it was surreal, but God, laughing with someone is good. Thank you Corinne, wherever you are. And thank you, Lucy.

25
SOCIAL STUDIES

Renate arranged for me to meet with a group of teachers and an assistant director of a small, privately funded school a short distance from where we were staying. It would be a valuable opportunity for me to learn from them. The visit centered around a presentation I agreed to make on recent trends in U.S. higher education, but I saw this as more of an exchange. That is exactly what it turned out to be. The group was small, as the meeting fell near the first of January when Haitians centered their attention on activities with family and friends. Plus it had come on the heels of a very wet spell when roads were at their muddiest and most difficult to travel. The founder of the school was away in Canada, his home country, on an educational tour, presumably with fundraising aspirations. Renate spoke very highly of his work and I could see how his vision influenced the creation of a high quality school staffed by excellent teachers.

When we entered the school grounds, the greenery was striking. We must have passed by this location before, as it was very near the doctor's house, but I could not have imagined that a school lay hidden beyond the road. Construction was underway for expansion. The original structure was limited in size but sturdy, constructed of cement block with three or four classrooms and an office surrounding a common area. The classrooms seated more students than would ever be expected in rooms of that size in the States, once more an indication that if you build a school they will come. The rooms were very dark, daylight inching in only through the rows of open-patterned block on one wall. The dimness was due also, I suppose, to the deep gray concrete floors, overcast skies, and dense tree cover on all sides of the building.

We pulled some desks together in the common area which, compared to the classrooms, felt more like an atrium. Light fell upon us through an opening in the ceiling, just enough to surround our circle. They apologized for the informality of our setting, but it was no less than perfect. I prefer to be seated when presenting to a small group, if the nature of the session allows. It did, and we had the most wonderful talk. We spoke about some of the challenges we face in education in our respective countries. I was in the midst of serving on the Indiana Commission for Higher Education, recently completing my time as a commissioner and having taken on responsibilities as chair of additional related committees. I used that as a framework. I had been a member of the Commission's Strategic Directions Committee and while what we addressed there might seem remote from what educators faced in Haiti, there were uncanny similarities. Though it was true that the scale of our challenges differed, the concerns remained the same.

Accessibility, affordability, accountability, college preparation, college completion, and clarifying missions of research institutions and community colleges were universal themes and easily introduced to this fertile, common ground. Those present were high school teachers and the exchange flowed with incredible ease. It has been my experience that when teachers meet with teachers, away from the demands and bureaucracy of daily work, they easily rekindle their passions and find common goals.

We spoke frankly about curriculum design and the desire for autonomy in the classroom while meeting standards determined elsewhere. In the United States those standards, at least in the public school system, are set at the state level. Working at the state level in post-secondary education matters I could see increasingly how our colleges and universities were under scrutiny in rising expectations for accountability.

Haiti's curricular decisions were centralized at the national level, in Port-au-Prince. While it made sense for a small country to rely on the efficiency that might come from coordinating efforts in the capital, the process was not always efficient. In the departments, or provinces, outside the capital the way of life and workforce development needs varied in countless ways, prompting teachers there to desire more power in curriculum development. Teachers did not object to infusing students with a traditional core of knowledge, but they wanted to enhance their programs based on local needs. In addition, what few resources were available in carrying out educational missions still were heavily concentrated in the capital.

For a myriad of reasons, Haiti did not have the capacity to build, staff, and maintain all of the schools that it needed. When individuals created schools they could do so with private donations and worked to see that their teachers were adequately prepared. This was necessary to maintain credibility and accountability to standards set in Port-au-Prince. These were not always easy to accomplish but the challenges did not deter philanthropists from erecting schools or teachers from teaching.

Those present at our gathering represented a number of disciplines. Still, I wanted to spend a bit more time speaking with the social studies instructor to learn what his expectations were and what his work was like. Having worked to prepare social studies teachers at my own campus, I knew something of state standards and found striking similarities. Very early in the primary grades children are introduced to ideas of community and eventually in the upper levels they come to learn geography and history that is more regional, national, and then global. The concepts emphasized in each country are similar – governments, democracy, independence, and so on. Sometimes it is impossible to imagine two more distinct countries than the United State and Haiti, but when we step back to take an honest look, we see how similar how similar our strategies and expectations are.

In the United States, our students and, still too often, teachers and professors, see the world from a perspective of U.S. exceptionalism – that our history, continued existence, and our frequent superiority in economics and war are reflections of our "specialness." This goes beyond an acknowledgement that the United States has exploited advantages or that it has used resources for its own gain. Rather, it suggests the nation has been "blessed" with advantages, indicating that they have come from a higher power. During the mid-19th century the concept of Manifest Destiny was used widely to prove that God had destined the United States to grow and prosper, and spread its influence from coast to coast. By the 1890s and beyond, U.S. influence reached elsewhere, many have said transforming its role from one of a republic to one of an empire.

In getting back to the basics of history, foundations, and social structures it is the idea of "republic" that should serve as the crux of our worldview. In doing so, we can see that our citizenship in a republic makes us more like Haitians than different from them. And sitting aside one another – U.S. teacher and Haitian teacher – in desks made for their students and more suitable and comfortable than can be imagined.

The United States and Haiti established themselves as independent republics, closer in history than perhaps any others. The two had been home to indigenous populations, had been explored and colonized by Europeans, and had developed with dependency on African slavery. Basing their arguments on Enlightenment principles of liberty and self-government, revolutionaries fought for representation within the empire and then for independence. Historical development from that point on took very different paths, but their constitutional foundations and struggle for world recognition shaped values taught to the children of each in very similar ways.

Our discussion that day turned to philosophies and purposes of education in a free society and ways in which we encourage students from elementary through middle school, high school, and into college to care about their nation's history and become more civically engaged. Gestures and body language became more vibrant and near electricity seemed to brighten the little daylight reaching from above.

"Isn't learning one's history integral to the molding of good citizens?" I asked.

"Yes!" he shouted. "Of course it is!"

"How can we live in a democratic society without it?"

"We can't."

"But how do we teach the truth about history? Does knowing the truth make the citizenry less patriotic?"

He sat back in his seat.

"It is a problem for us."

"It is a problem for us, too," I assured him. We further discussed differences between citizenship and patriotism, at one point questioning whether it was a school's responsibility to teach patriotism at all.

"We need to teach the truth," he said.

"I like to see young children who are proud of their country and I am not sure at what age they are ready to learn the truth." He smiled and nodded. His eyes cast down on his hands with a knowing look. He had clearly thought of these things, as well.

Also in the group was a math teacher. In addition to teaching, Henri did administrative work at the school. He described the growth in enrollment and said the school currently served 52 students from the ages of 12 to 20. Having taught math for several years at other schools, he seemed to make the transition to administration well. I asked him about it. He said much of his time is used to develop files on the children – one for each – to record academic progress and any disciplinary actions taken. The founder of the school insisted on maintaining high quality instruction and has required higher level systemization and assessment. At the very least this requires good record keeping. Henri added that he not only has set the tone for discipline among students, but also among the teachers. As he continued talking, my mind turned to what the possibilities of that might mean and I regret not asking for more explanation.

Henri was good at math, so he became a math teacher. The case with many Haitian teachers is that their ability in one subject area or another is noticed by one of their own teachers who recommend that they consider teaching themselves. For Henri, there were few other options in Jeremie, so teaching math it was. There was a polytechnic school nearby and he took advantage of it. The school offered no formal courses in pedagogy, but it was common for Haitians to teach with no formal training in education. Henri noted that there was now a law school in Jeremie affiliated with Seton Hall University and he hoped to complete a certification program there. What seems to be the case in Haiti is that where there is a school students will attend.

More students would attend at higher levels if it were possible. The transition from primary school to secondary school is a difficult one. Not necessarily because parents feel primary education is sufficient or that there is a sudden shift in the cost of an education at that point, both of which are true in many other countries. Rather, the entrance exam acts as an obstacle for most. First, only half of Haiti's children attend any sort of school at all so those who enter the formal education system are essentially privileged and eventually destined to complete as much as possible. In other words, those who are fortunate enough to attend school are already comparatively few, so this selectivity might insure greater success. However, the entrance exams for entering into secondary school – the equivalent of combined middle and high schooling in the U.S. system – are difficult. Only one percent of those who take the exam pass it. Even at that, disparity in levels of preparation, according to Henri, poses what he considers one of the biggest challenges for secondary school teachers.

Though not what one would consider "called" to the profession through vocation, Henri seemed as passionate about math as any teacher I have known. He looked on when the conversation had centered on civics as if it were the most important subject a child could learn. I assured him we shared a common respect for math. It pains me when I hear a student say they chose history as a major because they were not good in math. I want them to choose history for better reasons than that. Plus, I would like everyone to work at being good in math.

"The Department of Mathematics is near my office on campus," I told him. "There are posters in the hallway that say, 'We all do math every day.'" He smiled at that as only a math teacher could.

"It is true!" he said. "We all do math every day!" I looked at the dark gray cement block walls around us and imagined colorful and inspirational posters about learning math. There were only a few small religious pictures and a calendar.

We reluctantly ended our meeting when it was time to go. They asked if I would like to take a look at the new construction on our way out.

"I would love to," I told them. The air was still damp from recent rains and we carefully stepped over mud that surrounded the concrete foundation. The outside walls of additional classrooms were up, and steel reinforcements jutted from the half-finished ceiling.

"These rooms will be much better, much stronger."

The older classrooms seemed perfectly stable to me, and they might have sufficed, except perhaps in the case of a natural disaster. They were far from the epicenter of the earthquake, but the images of steel reinforcements were etched in my mind. I later wished very much that the vulnerable schools in Port-au-Prince had been constructed in such a manner.

26
LOW TOWN

Basse-Ville is a section of Jeremie that lies directly on the Caribbean. Renate took me there on a school visit that turned out to be more inspiring than I could imagine. Americans consider waterfront properties the most desirable and assume that it must be the case in the Caribbean, but it is not so. Historically waterfront sections of cities have been home to outcasts – the poor, unskilled, immigrants and so on. They were typically walled off; often physically and always socially. In Jeremie, a small port city already struggling economically, the people of Basse-Ville were further neglected.

From the water's edge, the narrow, pebbled beach slants up to a stone barrier that meets the edge of a narrow two-lane road. From there, living quarters are stacked up the hill, overlooking the sea. Fishermen cast and drag nets, wading waist-deep not far from the shore. The water is gray, yet it glistens when sunlight peers through the clouds. The beach is gray, too. Kids run barefoot, frequently kicking soccer balls. Goats, pigs, chickens and an occasional donkey walk along the road. More kids stand watching whatever passes their way. Many wear t-shirts sized far too large and sometimes nothing else. The houses are small and dark, and rise steeply. They lie close together and although considered home and made as comfortable as possible are less inviting than the outdoors. A child occasionally crosses the road to empty a bucket of human waste into the sea. This is a crowded neighborhood of 5,000 with no plumbing.

"Is it really like they show on TV?" I am sometimes asked after returning from an underdeveloped area in Latin America.

"Is what like they show on TV?" I respond, though I'm pretty sure I know what they've seen.

"All those children. Living with nothing."

"Sometimes." Images of Basse-Ville come to mind, but not in the ways that television fundraisers present. The children do not stare at me with hunger in their eyes as if they want something from me. They go about their daily activities, which might mean dumping the family urine and excrement, followed by a game of barefoot soccer on a pebbly beach. I am essentially irrelevant to them.

There was a moment while stopped on the road that day, perhaps for a pig or goat crossing, when a young boy smiled at me, came close to the truck, and reached inside the window to touch my hair. He caught me off guard. The curiosity and fearlessness among children never cease to amaze me. A white child who has never encountered a black woman might reach to touch her hair. That is if the natural tendency toward curiosity and fearlessness had not been damaged in some way. When my daughter was in preschool, she had a good friend who was black. One night after bedtime stories and before lights out, she struck up a conversation about her classmates.

"Sola's hands are always dirty," she noted matter-of-factly.

"What do you mean?" I knew who Sola was.

"He washes and washes, but they're still the same color."

"That is the color of his skin."

"Oh." She transitioned to another subject, but I stayed on this one, believing more explanation was in line. The historian in me no doubt provided more information than was necessary for a 3-year-old. I was not sure how the idea of dirt arose in her mind or why the color of his hands might be construed as something negative. I am not an expert in those things, and my kids have since informed me that people my age overthink race and ethnicity, as if we are trying to overcompensate for something. It is incredible how much things can change in one generation. When I was about 4 or 5, I first came face-to-face with a black boy just about my size in a department store during my family's annual Easter shopping trip. My mother somehow managed to come up with play clothes for us, sewed some dresses for regular Sundays, and made sure we had all the pieces to our school uniforms. Easter shopping with my father was a real event. We were treated to gloves, hats, anklets, shoes, and coats – the whole deal.

Once my selections were made and attention turned toward my sisters', I ran up and down aisles running my hands along sleeves as if they were slats in a picket fence. I heard someone in the next aisle doing the same and as we met at the end we stopped dead, our eyes locking. He was just my height. It must have been around 1962. My family lived in a white suburb about five miles or so from Gary and I am not sure what I had learned about race up until that point. I wanted to touch him and I think he, me, but our parents called us away from each other. The Haitian child touching my hair somehow satisfied a need to complete that interaction.

Not only are the residents of Basse-Ville isolated from the world, they are isolated from rest of their own city. It took the special energy, time, and attention a few have invested to make a difference in their lives. One such person was Pierre. About 15 years earlier, he and a friend acknowledged a need for a school there, but they had nothing to give but their time. He told me that the children were considered unworthy of an education. The light in his eyes told me he could never consider any child unworthy of an education. He and his friend started a school with seven students and no building. They sat on rocks and learned.

In 2004, when tensions surrounding the presidency were growing, the Grand'Anse population was primarily pro-Aristide. Far from the capital, the economic and policy-making center, these two practical idealists of the Grand'Anse worked to carryout Aristide's mission of empowering the poor. Despite criticism, they remained true to his vision. As the forced removal of Aristide neared, the lives of his public supporters were in danger. The close friend of Pierre, and co-founder of this small school, was murdered. Stunned and wondering what they future might hold Pierre decided to move forward with their plans to keep the dream alive. A clearly spiritual man, he acknowledged that a faith in God had aided in moving the project forward.

Today the school is truly a school, a three-story concrete structure with a growing faculty that serves more than 700 students. The day I was able to visit was a quiet one and school was not in session. As a result, I was able to sit and converse with three amazing and inspiring educators, Pierre and two members of the teaching staff, in an empty classroom. Caribbean waves lapped the shore across the road. The large window openings allowed for a warm, refreshing breeze and I wondered again how it could possibly be January.

Pierre and his colleagues took time to detail the workings of the school. The size of the student population required staggered starting times: 7:00 a.m. for 6th-9th grades, 8:00 a.m. for 1st-5th grades, and 8:30 a.m. for preschool. Mid-morning marked recreation time and a meal of mixed grain. Attendance was generally good, they reported, with students traveling anywhere from a few minutes to nearly two hours from home. Student fees ran 200 *gourdes* per year for 1st-5th grades. This was the equivalent of 4 or 5 dollars and they could not always pay, meaning teachers did not always get paid. Still, teachers continued to teach, likely due to their dedication to student learning, but also through Pierre's inspiration. He had undying faith that the school would succeed.

At the conclusion of 6th and 9th grades, students were required to take rigorous national exams, and the school boasted a 90 percent pass rate. But administering the exams posed its own set of problems. Technology and teaching materials were hard to come by. That is why I was especially grateful and honored that Pierre parted with a textbook, which he gave to me as a gift. Having it in my hands was not something I took lightly.

27
TEXTBOOKS

Being able to spend some time with a textbook allowed me to more carefully compare and contrast it with those used in U.S. classrooms. The similarities were striking, but so, too, were the differences. Some of what set this one apart was not so much what makes it uniquely Haitian, but what makes it clearly not of the U.S.

What was given to me was a 9th year social sciences text, authored by Carltz Docteur, Professor of Social Sciences, whose degree was earned at L'Lecole Normal Superieure. It was entitled *Quelques Grandes Etapes, Dans L'Evolution de L'Humanité* and it contained significant history of the world from the 18th through the 20th centuries. The subject matter was not presented in linear, chronological order. Rather, it explored various themes within the social sciences and detailed historical developments and players through examples. The physical quality was not great, reflecting the lack of resources in the country. It used only the most basic paper and ink printing processes, and the type formatting was not very polished. It resembled what, in the U.S., might be published as a workbook – or "consumable" as they are known in the field – in decades past. But the content was substantive and impressive, as well as impressionistic.

It is impossible for survey textbooks to delve into subjects with adequate depth. That is not their nature. But this one gave quick glimpses of an approach to history distinct from what was seen in the United States. First, the cover design included a map of Haiti and portraits of the following admired leaders: Franklin Delano Roosevelt, Charles de Gaulle, Winston Churchill, Toussaint L'Ouverture, and Che Guevara. The introductory chapter on "Human Societies" grounded the modern world in the history of independence from England, as well as from Spain, Portugal and France, noting that colonial abuses were best articulated by Thomas Jefferson and Thomas Paine. The Monroe Doctrine earned a prominent place, as did a map illustrating "North American Domination in Latin America."

A brief timeline of the "World since 1960" included only the following: Decolonization of Africa (1945-1975), Cuban Crisis (October 1962), Beginning of Détente (1963), First Oil Shock (1961-1973), Rise of Islam (1976), Communist Victories in Indochina (1975), Khomeini Ascension to Power in Iran (1979), Falklands War [Malvinas] (1982). The Cold War was given approximately two paragraphs. The decolonization of Africa was given approximately four and a half pages. The section on Caribbean abolition history includes the following timeline: Saint Domingue [Haiti] (1793), Santo Domingo (1822), British Colonies of the West Indies [eastern islands and Jamaica, Trinidad, Honduras, and British Guyana] (1833-1838), French Colonies [Guadeloupe, Martinique, French portion of St. Martin and French Guyana] (1848); Dutch Colonies [Curacao, Bonaire, Aruba, Saba, Saint-Eustache, Dutch portion of St. Martin, and Dutch Guyana] (1863), Puerto Rico (1873), and Cuba (1886). The section on Caribbean independence included the following timeline: Haiti (1804), Dominican Republic (1844), Cuba (1898), Jamaica (1962), Barbados (1966), Grenada (1974), Dominica (1978), St. Vincent and the Grenadines (1979), St. Lucia (1979), Antigua (1981), and St. Kitts and Nevis (1983).

Within the section devoted to Antillean society, Haiti played a prominent role, with attention devoted to French colonialism, slave revolts, enfranchisement, constitutional processes, agrarian regimes, and international relations, or lack thereof. The section on Haitian society re-emphasized revolutionary ideals of independence and stages of development in early nationhood. It also defined more clearly the concepts of the state, the nation, the nation-state, and nationalism. This chapter's glossary contained such entries as autocrat, conservatism, despotism, liberalism, political liberty, oligarchy, pluralism, and separation of powers. Following the chapters more conventionally formatted to address history was one examining global economic disparity and the conditions of the Third World. Topics addressed included agricultural land development, famine, malnutrition, literacy, birth rates, and environmental protection.

The author noted two primary economic systems in the world – capitalism and socialism – and in straightforward terms went on to describe each. He used concepts such as modes of production, work and capital, the law of supply and demand, productivity and efficiency research, and economic planning. In the last chapters, current conditions in the Caribbean and then Haiti were examined in this context, while emphasizing the roles that global capitalism, neo-colonialism, and more powerful countries had played. From a U.S. perspective, the work may seem biased, but a closer examination of curriculum and textbooks used in the U.S. demonstrate comparable biases. Yes, Haiti's are Haitian-centric. In looking at histories of the world written in different countries we can also see that those of the U.S. are U.S.-centric.

I did not plan to meet with a textbook publisher in Haiti, but fortunate circumstances permitted it to happen. After completing work in Jeremie we returned to Port-au-Prince (my suitcase was waiting for me at the airport) and learned there was a new publisher of textbooks living in Petionville. A friend of Renate knew of him, and he graciously agreed to meet with me. We followed the directions given to us and found ourselves entering the world of Haiti's elite. A very long driveway led up a hill to his home; the gated property protected by an armed security guard. His home was spectacular and we met on the marble-tiled patio where we were served tea and cookies. Perfectly manicured blooming vines and hanging baskets surrounded us. His pet dogs joined us. He was the perfect host.

His company was called Editions Zémès, and he showed me some of his work. There was no need for Renate to assist in interpreting; his English was perfect. He told me he produced educational materials in a wide range of subjects but knew I was interested in the social sciences. Simply prototypes at this point but soon to be available in schools, the books were beautiful in contrast to what I had seen. The quality of materials, writing, illustrations, and photograph reproductions were comparable to those of the latest textbooks in the United States. Some years before, I had served on a parent advisory committee for textbook selection for my children's school and visited a social studies textbook exposition where publishers and sales representatives put forth their best new work. I told him his materials were just as good. He was very pleased. But I wondered who in Haiti could afford them.

We began to talk more specifically about content, and how history is taught in the schools. Again, this was an exhilarating exchange. We spoke to centrism and patriotism and truth, and the value of including Caribbean history in the world's story. I told him of recent efforts to recognize Haiti's role as an essential component in teaching the Revolutionary Era. He nodded with enthusiasm and grinned.

"It is so true!" he agreed.

"I want to do my best to include it," I assured him. Ideas of education were integral to that story, as well. Historically, Haitian educators were torn between infusing a sense of culture and philosophical thought parallel to curriculum found in French models or adopting the English model of "useful" learning. The elite of Haiti were educated the French way and at higher levels their children sent to study abroad. Before the Revolution, Haiti was considered primarily a slave colony and the idea of educating slaves posed a myriad of concerns. What purpose would it serve to educate anyone who was destined for a life of manual labor? The investment required seemed hardly worth considering. The cost of constructing schools and paying teachers' salaries would not have been prohibitive in this most profitable of France's colonies; however, financial investment in the education of others' children sparked debates everywhere in the modern world at the time of the Enlightenment. In the case of manual laborers it hardly seemed a good investment, especially if it meant introducing them to ideas of liberty and human rights so much a part of Enlightenment philosophy.

The Revolutionary Era saw a transformation in the philosophy of education. Discussions of John Locke's concept of the *tabula rasa* described in his *An Essay Concerning Human Understanding* were making their way into sophisticated circles. He argued that parents and teachers should take greater care to recognize how much children were shaped by experience, giving them both greater power and responsibility in purposefully creating the kinds of adults future societies would want to see. Thomas Jefferson's vision, though incomplete with regard to those of African descent, embraced the idea of the perfectibility of man, acknowledging that education could play a greater role in recognizing the potential among more of the population. It would ultimately serve not only the individual well, but also society at large. Again, the main purpose of Haitian slaves was to provide manual labor, and that took little education. The French considered this new Anglo-influenced approach as too utilitarian but as Haiti entered a new era of independence educating for the future was embraced. Through the centuries, curriculum and textbooks have reflected both.

I came away with many things that day, not the least of which was a better understanding of the class system in Haiti. While much of the upper class turns away to the needs of the population's majority, he did not. He could have remained closed off in his mansion, living very well without working. Instead, he chose to risk starting a publishing company to improve the education of the country's youth.

I also learned from speaking to him, as well at the educators in the Grand'Anse, just how strong their commitment to social studies education was. This is what I suspected, but interacting with them help to reinforce it. Too often, people from the outside view Haitians as pitiable and living in abject circumstances. While it is true that Haitians have met with more than their fair share of challenges, far too many underestimate their capacity to envision a better future and take matters into their own hands if given the means to do so.

28
HOSPICE ST. JOSEPH

Each morning and evening at Hospice St. Joseph we stood to sing the meal prayer. Picking up a tune has never come easy for me and the words were in Creole, but I did my best.

"*Mesi, Papa . . .*"

Our Haitian hosts were gracious, but their knowing grins suggested a bit of pleasure in watching us butcher something so common to them, also in seeing Americans reminded to be grateful for the food we were about to eat. Simple as that. How many of us were taught at a very young age to say grace and have long since lost the habit? The Hospice meals were always perfect – perfectly prepared, perfectly presented, perfectly healthy. At the start of each day it brought us to a place of mindfulness and thoughtful preparation for what we might encounter that day. In the streets of Port-au-Prince, that might be anything. At the end of each day the meal prayer and nourishment reinforced an appreciation for our blessings. In teaching us the meal prayer there was no formal instruction, only its word printed on a wall plaque. As with many singing rituals there was merely an expectation that one join in. So we did.

On the nights when I was the sole guest at Hospice, there was just myself and one host, at least in material form.

There seemed to be a greater power there, as well, or the spirit of the religious life I was introduced to as a child. I realized that my faith in something non-material had not totally disappeared. The table of dark, heavy wood, in a dimly lit room of green walls with crosses and other religious images watching over me was reminiscent of my grandmother's dining room. Hers was graced with a large, heavy table covered in plastic lace, statues of Our Lady of the Snows and the Sacred Heart of Jesus, and a 12 by 28 or so replica of DaVinci's "Last Supper" on the wall. On decorative stands and dressers there were holy cards, novena calculations, and books on the lives of the saints. Long after she died I came to understand the challenges she had faced in raising ten children with no steady income from my grandfather, and it made more sense why she might spend so much time praying for miracles. Similar images adorned the dining room in Port-au-Prince. How could I not feel the presence of God or see a glimpse of a culture so reliant on praying for miracles?

Behind my place at the table hung a figure worked in metal. During one meal with others present it was quite the topic of conversation. Was it an angel? Was it not an angel? The artistic representation of this figure was striking. Long, flowing dress, trees, birds and other symbols of nature, and wild, wild hair. The hair was in braids, or dreadlocks, or snakes. Whatever they were, they gave her something special.

The other guests that day were two women about my age, one a doctor and one a nun. They lived in two separate southern states – Louisiana and Florida, I believe – and made frequent trips to Haiti to provide medical care. It was apparent to me that they were soul mates of some kind, joined in spirit. They admitted before I said a word that people generally believed they must have known each other forever, but that they had met only a few years before. They were committed, however, to meeting regularly to continue their work in Haiti together.

Their eyes lit up as they shared stories of serving children. It was evident they were destined to meet. In looking at them I wondered if this was one of the ways in which God worked on earth – through putting people together to accomplish what needed to be done. Their relationship was clearly greater than the sum of its parts and they would be the first to admit it.

They laughed so much in unison that it was infectious and told a story of how they almost did not make it to Port-au-Prince. Their plane was paralyzed by ice, much in the way mine had been, but Baton Rouge airport personnel were inexperienced in matters of wintry weather and ill-equipped to respond.

"Even the de-icing truck was frozen," said the doctor.

"Can you imagine?" said the nun, chiming in. The country had been experiencing frightening changes in the weather.

Compounding their delay was the discovery that their airline had revised its baggage limits since their last trip.

"We brought suitcases of medicine, but had to empty everything in the airport and repack the best we could."

"We're praying that what we left behind will make it here on its own." I nodded, hesitant to tell them I had had baggage troubles of my own.

The doctor believed the hair of the metal-worked woman was not intended to represent anything wild about this female figure – simply that it was being carried by the wind. We looked more carefully. There was no mistaking she had something coming from her shoulders – something suggesting wings. Perhaps she was an angel. But they were not so massive as to make her clearly one; not wings that one might see on a Western European or American Christmas card. No. These were small and leaf-like. They might have been leaves. In a way they intertwined with the nature scene of which she was part. If angels and all beings are part of one world, the world of nature, the world of spirit, the world of Haiti, the world of us all, then why couldn't they be both leaves and wings – wings of leaves – on a woman whose hair was one with the wind?

It was among the most extraordinary of breakfast conversations I ever had. The others excused themselves to begin their day in the community. I looked at her again and then turned around. A beautiful and delicate figure crafted of the earth's elements she granted me permission to be of the natural world and the spiritual world, of country, of humanity, of femininity, of earth, sky, water and air. I felt comforted sensing her on the wall behind me. She had my back.

29
LAST DAY

Renate took me to an artisans' cooperative on our last day in Port-au-Prince. She was familiar with the work for sale there and had promised to bring some painted crosses to a friend for a Catholic social organization fundraiser back home. The building sat back from the sidewalk in a nice area, surrounded by well-maintained landscaping. I took a mental picture knowing I would be returning to a Chicago winter blast the following afternoon.

We parked close to the curb and a man approached us, his arms overflowing with colorful doll-like figures he was selling. Renate smiled at him and suggested I buy one. He returned her smile, as if they had known each other for some time.

"He makes these to support his family," she whispered to me.

I looked at the figures more closely, and they did not resemble any type of dolls I had seen before. They were made of wrapped, thin straw dyed vivid shades of orange, pink and red. The wide brims of their hats were made of twisted braids, their faces of black cloth each with two simple stitches for eyes and one for a mouth. A bundle of bright straw of about six or seven inches in length fanned into full length skirts resembling small hand brooms. From the torso and waist down, they vaguely reminded me of the yarn dolls my sisters and I made at day camp.

Renate spoke to the man briefly in Creole and then turned to me.

"They're two for a dollar," she said.

I bought two, not only because they were such a bargain but because they captivated me. I chose a pair in contrasting colors, one with an orange bodice and red skirt, the other with a red bodice and orange skirt. Both wore pink hats. I cradled them gently as we stepped up the walk.

"Do you know what they are?" Renate asked. I wasn't sure. The brush my Aunt Jeannette used to clean the table after cookies and milk came to mind. I told her so.

"That is exactly what they are."

Aunt Jeannette subtly tried to educate us about the finer things – soft-boiled egg cups, sweater clips, the importance of wearing a slip – I suppose to prepare us for marriage to sophisticated husbands one day. When she died, somewhere in the process of dividing up her things I was given her crumb brush. These were quite different, but I liked how Haitians maintained that sense of propriety, using tablecloths and taking the time to brush the crumbs away after each meal.

In the shop, I looked at shelves and shelves of handmade items. It was difficult to limit my purchase to just a few things. Each held a certain degree of energy, and I wanted to spend some time in their midst. Whether completely unique or in stacks of dozens, each came into existence through human imagination, circumstance, and touch. Standing near a piece, it might exude warmth, the creative energy of human mind and body lingering. Stepping back to take in a work in its entirety can remind a person that there is a creator attached.

There were earrings, wall hangings, textiles, and painted greeting cards. I settled on a pair of trivets. Well, trivets more or less, as they were legless and made of woven rattan. Perhaps hot pads would better describe them. They seemed charming yet useful for the kitchen and served to sustain my cross-cultural bond with women everywhere who prepare food for their families. In bringing food from the oven to the table I would be reminded of the challenge of doing so elsewhere in the world. I also bought a cross of metalwork paint with faces of every color, and planned to hang it next to one of wood I had earlier brought home from El Salvador. And finally, I chose a bracelet, as I had in other countries in the past.

Wearing a bracelet brought from Latin America serves as the best reminder of what I have experienced as I go on with my day-to-day life back home. It is so easy to lose touch with our experiences once we return to our work and families. Photographs are stored, with perhaps a few displayed in dens or offices. Art is framed for walls and sculptures placed on tables, but after walking past them repeatedly as weeks and months go by they can become invisible and forgotten.

A bracelet, however, is more present. The work that we do in the world – which in my case might include typing at the computer, writing on a chalkboard, or handing back exams – can bring a bracelet into plain sight many times a day. My wrists are small, so whether of beads, wood, or knotted string, the bracelet often dangles, forcing me to adjust it with the fingers of my other hand. What might seem a nuisance to some is a nudge for me to be continually grateful. It brings less developed Latin America into focus and to my touch. What I share with students through books, films, and my own interpretations becomes more tangible. It is a reminder of why I do what I do. If I should ever complain while I am wearing one – that I am not paid enough, that I have not yet had time for lunch, that I am underappreciated – I take a moment to hold my wrist and remember how fortunate I am.

This time I chose one of marbled plastic. I am sorry to say that it broke in half within a couple weeks. The stress of returning to daily activities post-earthquake manifested itself in strange ways. As I took it from my nightstand one morning and began to put it on, it snapped in my hand.

30
LAST NIGHT

I admit to having spent much time attempting to recreate my last experiences in Haiti before the earthquake in order to make better sense of things. Looking back on leaving a city that was comparatively intact and then in ruins, it would have felt good to say, "Well, at least I did this" or "At least I did that" as if some type of meaningful action, no matter how large or small, might have done some lasting good. If I had put the finishing touches on a significant project, or even held the hand of a Haitian child one last time, my being there might somehow have been more worthwhile. Deep down I knew the destruction might have made any additional acts of kindness irrelevant. The country would be forever changed due to the disaster. So I suppose it was ok that I spent my last evening in Port-au-Prince watching a movie. Not just any movie, mind you. I watched *The Hangover*.

I don't usually spend time watching television or films while abroad. I find it best to stay in the moment, to experience every possible real life experience – tasting the tastes, smelling the smells, and interacting with human beings in all likelihood I will never see again. To be immersed in a different culture for even a brief time, gives one more time to acknowledge what about it is so "foreign." It also helps us to acknowledge the strangeness of lifestyles and values from one's own culture from the outside. Watching *The Hangover* in Port-au-Prince was surreal and might have served as a serious reminder of the decadent excess that is America, if I had not been laughing so hard.

"My mother would never watch this," said one of the graduate students staying at Hospice St. Joseph. "It's cool that you find it funny." I wanted so much not to find it funny. I had heard about it and seeing it with my own eyes made it a bit worse, and would have even more so, if the film had not been so good. I stopped cringing early on as I doubled over in laughter.

Perhaps it was the beer. The television and DVD player were situated in an open-aired common area with a view of the city. The space was furnished with comfortable chairs and a refrigerator stocked with Coca Cola and Prestige, the local brew. Nearby were a bottle opener and a box for payment – one dollar each. I had not had a beer in some time and it took only a couple to help me enjoy *The Hangover* even more. The professor accompanying the class exhibited more restraint, but these were not my students. They were enrolled in a health care administration program at a university in Colorado and had been touring the country to get a closer look at the state of medicine in Haiti. They were an eclectic group and I tried to imagine them working as administrators down the road.

Their professor was an expert in global health care delivery and he was taking them to clinics and hospitals, meeting with them at the end of each day for class discussion and deliberation of case studies. At that point, they were the only other guests at Hospice and I felt a guest among them as we shared breakfast and dinner my last few days in Port-au-Prince. Internet service was available there, so I could busy myself with my laptop in my room, or sit on the balcony with the warm breeze helping me to forget it was winter. My Facebook friends reported details of a snowstorm pelting Chicago. I wondered whether there was any sort of shovel in the trunk of my car I imagined it being slowly buried in the parking lot of the airport shuttle.

No matter, I thought. There was nothing I could do about it. I might as well enjoy the early evening sunset and the downtime. I thought it great that the students invited me to watch a film on my last night there. They had more work to do in the morning, but I was packed and looking forward to getting home and preparing for the new semester. I could not wait to share my wonderful experiences with a new group of students, letting them know that Haiti was making forward strides, however small, and a positive feeling seemed to permeate the population. Things were not all bad, and taking time to laugh seemed an appropriate close to a rewarding visit.

31
EARTHLY SENSITIVITIES

The rooster crows of that night were like none I had ever heard. They were constant and unceasing.

In visiting the Caribbean I had become accustomed to the sounds of roosters. In the Grand'Anse they woke me like clockwork. It was a good thing, too, as the losing of luggage left me without any way of telling time. My limited understanding of cellular technology allowed me to figure out only that the alarm function on my phone did not work because I did not have service in Haiti. I set the alarm anyway, with the hope that some satellite would magically target my location and provide whatever was necessary to wake me on time. I was grateful for the roosters.

The wonders of technology never cease to amaze me and I am content with the fact that they remain wonders for me. I try not to take them for granted for then they might transform from enhancing my life to making me dependent. I like that they can help me and am forever appreciative. But I am comforted in knowing that I can get through life on pre-technology basics. And that goes over well in Haiti.

I suppose that is the former Girl Scout in me. I can start a fire if I have to, sail against the wind, find the North Star, apply a tourniquet, and even suck the venom from a snake bite. I am definitely somebody I can depend on. But non-technology life also includes paying closer attention to the natural world and what it can offer us. In the case of the Grand'Anse roosters, they were able to wake me on time, even early. Having no alarm or cell service did not matter.

Roosters are commonplace in Caribbean cities as well as in the countryside. They play significant cultural roles in cockfighting and syncretic religion, as well as egg fertilization. The same may be true in urban neighborhoods of the United States where island immigrants have settled. Local ordinances are difficult to enforce and newcomers may be resistant to letting go of familiar rituals. In the States, most of us no longer are so close to our food that we raise chickens. But that was not always the case. My mother used to tell stories of her childhood in the 1940s when my grandfather raised chickens – along with his victory garden – in their yard, with a coop he fashioned in the garage. Fresh eggs were a staple, and he occasionally butchered a chicken for dinner.

"Do you know what it means to run around like a chicken with its head cut off?" my mother once asked me. When we were growing up, she openly shared information about the things she knew.

"Like crazy?" I guessed.

"Just flopping around with no direction, no sense," she said. "I've seen it with my own eyes. My father would chop the head off, but the chicken wouldn't die right away. It would just run around the yard a bit, until it fell over." It was hard to get the image out of my head.

My mom did not generally dwell on gruesomeness or boast of experiencing such things. She was just matter-of-fact about it. She is one of the most genuinely kind people I have ever met and she did not purposely try to get a rise out of us.

She just wanted to pass on the knowledge. She was always pretty comfortable around food animals. She could clean fish and stuff sausage casings without batting an eye. She was not sadistic about it, or squeamish. She was just good about being in touch with her food. I romanticized her life as a young girl with the sounds of downtown Hammond, Indiana not yet silenced by the demise of Great Lakes urban economies and still enhanced by roosters waking her in the morning.

In the rural Caribbean, animal sounds fill the air. People there are close to their food, and it is not uncommon to see chickens walking the property, in and out of homes, in and out of kitchens. To be served poultry or eggs in their presence can be unnerving at first, but one gets used to it. In Haiti they are often thin, having subsisted on limited feed. Knowing I could learn to accept food that had once been alive under my feet, I wondered whether I could witness the slaughter. There were times when I was tempted to ask local cooks whether it was really true that chickens could run around with their heads cut off. It was not as if I doubted my mother's word. I was just curious.

The use of chickens and/or roosters in voodoo rituals is even more a mystery to me. I do know their blood is used though I have not witnessed it myself, at least in person. A friend of mine who consulted with a practitioner of Santería near Chicago confided that she once underwent a "cleansing" that involved the use of a chicken. She left it at that, knowing I would probably not want to hear any more. In the documentary on voodoo I showed to my class, a chicken's neck was slit, just enough to cast droplets of blood across a person in need of healing. Understanding that much made me think twice when I heard crowing, particularly in urban communities home to Caribbean immigrants.

These are the images that circled through my mind as I lay awake that night, listening to their incessant cries. I also reflected on the fact that I took only a few photographs in my entire time there. I took one of a metal-worked art piece in the gift shop at Hospice. It was of the sun and moon depicted in a way similar to the *yin* and *yang* of Taoism, and reminded me so much of the man I still held in my heart. I fantasized that we complemented one another that way, and remembered him telling me in a phone call from California that he found sun and moon tiles to grace the fireplace in the bedroom of his new house. I knew that the piece would not fit in my suitcase and I knew that having it would only delay the inevitability of letting him go once and for all. But a picture seemed harmless.

I also took two photographs from my balcony of some boys playing in front of the small store across the street. Together they summarize why I hesitate to take photos there. To capture images of people is to capture so much that is wonderful about Haiti. But it can also put the photographer into the position of gawker. It is best to ask permission to take a photo of someone and even then it makes me uneasy, imagining how I would feel if someone from a foreign country stopped me on the street at home to take a picture. In a deeper exchange between people it can interrupt the flow of friendship or association, but boys horsing around while they purchased a Coca-Cola depicted a simple moment of pleasure, and I thought I would go unnoticed. They did not see me while I took the first, but in the second one of the younger ones stared up at me as if to ask why I thought I had a right to do that.

The last couple of photographs I took were of the sun setting on the hills of Port-au-Prince. It was gorgeous. My thoughts turned to those hills and the crowing exchange that continued as they darkened. I wondered about the likelihood of cockfighting in the area, so prevalent in the islands. When I commented to someone on the strength of the crowing, I was told it was due to the roosters being bred for lives of competition. It showed in their communication. They were expressing voices of oneupsmanship.

But that was not enough to explain what I heard in the night hours preceding the earthquake. Hospice St. Joseph sat high and the balcony outside my room looked out over the city to the west. On previous evenings I had watched the sunset – one of the most beautiful I had ever seen – hills lying to the left and to the right. They were densely populated with people living in concrete block homes, some having lived there for generations, many more having come there in recent decades. The beauty of the early evening sky cast the dwellings in a whole new light. Up close, their lives seemed unimaginably hard. From a distance, they were peaceful – quietly settled amidst the dark hills and bathed in glorious colors known only at the end of the day.

The daytime rooster crows of the city often go unnoticed as traffic and the noises of work and play take the stage. But in a city where only a small percentage have access to electricity, activity dies down with the setting of the sun and the occasional honk of a horn or shout to a friend begins to stand out. So, too, do the sounds of the animals. When thinking back, I remembered hearing sounds of dogs during previous evenings, barking back and forth from hillside to hillside. And I remembered hearing roosters, too. But nowhere near what I heard during the night before the earthquake. The crowing went on all night long.

Perhaps I slept lighter knowing I had a few last minute tasks to take care of in the morning. My driver was scheduled to pick me up around 9:00 or 9:30 and it is never easy for me to sleep soundly the night before a trip. Still, the sounds were greater than that. And they were nonstop.

"Er-er-er-er-errrr!" one would wail.

"Er-er-er-er-errrr!" another would carry on.

It was not so much that they were competing. This was not oneupsmanship. It was as if they were carrying a message as far as they possibly could – one to the next from my hillside to the next and the next and the next. Then, before continuing far into the distance, back again. They were not replying to one another as much as they were spreading the word.

God, just let me sleep, I thought. I did not know what had provoked them, but their cries clearly differed from those of previous nights.

Only sometime after the earthquake did I think again about that night, and wonder whether they knew something we did not. In following months there emerged an interesting discussion on an internet social network devoted to nature. A researcher was seeking input on how the animal world might be tuned in to natural disasters. I reported my experience, and was assured that the roosters undoubtedly sensed what was happening under the earth. If only we had know what they were trying to say.

The drive to the airport was one I will remember always. The morning air was clear and crisp. The sun shone. People sold their wares along the streets. Others boarded *tap taps* for work and shopping. Children smiled on their way to school. I leaned on my arm, resting on the open window of the truck, and took mental pictures of everything I saw. I considered taking the camera from my purse but decided against it. Life was getting better for the people of Port-au-Prince. They seemed at peace and full of hope. Things were moving forward little by little and I did not want to intervene in any way with

the click of a shutter button. When I landed at O'Hare news of
the earthquake sharpened those images.

32
ADJUSTMENT

The next day I returned to my office. Part of my intention in being there was to establish some sort of normalcy, but I also needed to prepare for the new semester, which was due to begin the following week. I had promised myself that my syllabi, assignments, and schedules would be completed before I left for Haiti, but I got caught up in the holiday rhythm and took the idea of a break from work to heart. This would not be the first time I was rushed to make course preparations in just days before the start of classes and I had taught these before.

But this time there was no sense of anticipation, no sense of excitement or pressure, no surge of adrenaline. Not a drop. I sat paralyzed at my desk. Before I had left for Port-au-Prince I planned to discuss Haiti with my classes at some point in coming weeks, and would work it into the semester schedule. I had made such reports on travels to other countries before. But now I felt as if I had nothing to say. There were no words to describe what I had experienced; what I was still experiencing. I did not even know what it was that I was experiencing.

My work e-mail inbox was full of messages. Limited internet access in Haiti had caused them to pile up. I dazedly scrolled through them. There was one from the University

Relations department that stood out. E-mails from that office are generally notices to the campus community describing recent press releases sent or activities coming up. But this one seemed to be addressed only to me. I wondered how they could be contacting me so quickly. I opened it.

Apparently the local newspaper was working to create a Spanish version of its weekend edition for the Hispanic community and a reporter wanted a comment about their new project from me. I had become known as the Latinamericanist, teaching everything from the Inca and Maya to recent Latino immigration trends in Indiana. I sat with my hands on the keyboard, not knowing at first how to reply. The weight that had settled over me was difficult to bear. I took a couple of shallow breaths and began to type.

"Hi , Wes. It sounds like a wonderful idea, but I'm not sure I will be able to talk with them right now. I just got back from Haiti yesterday. There was an earthquake. Kathy." Of course, he must have heard about the earthquake, but I could not find any more words.

When I ran into my colleagues they had varying reactions. Some had not heard that I was in Haiti and engaged in normal, everyday conversation as if nothing had happened. It was just as well. I wanted so much for work to be normal. A few others stared with pained expressions, not knowing what to say. I nodded and introduced topics unrelated to anything they had expected. Still others stopped dead in their tracks and told me how happy they were to see me.

"It's horrible what happened in Haiti. Just horrible," lamented an academic advisor in the hallway near the technology labs.

"Yes," I replied.

"I can't believe it. Have you been watching the news?"

"Yes."

"Of course, you have. Is it true you barely got out? Were you close to that area?

"Well…"

"That's what I heard. I just can't believe it. Can't believe it."

People who worked in administration began contacting me. I knew the campus rumor mill was swift and hearty, but I was surprised this was even on their radar. Evidently a number of key players were in a meeting when someone noted I had been in Haiti and suggested I did not get out in time.

"Don't you remember that you had scheduled a later flight and then changed it?" the Dean's assistant reminded me.

"Uh… " I had forgotten that I initially planned to leave in the early evening, but realized I rarely get anything substantial accomplished on a travel day, so I might as well rebook my flight for morning.

"I still had the original paperwork and so did West Lafayette. We thought you were still there and couldn't get out!"

The university system had implemented a process by which the main campus was notified when any faculty member traveled to a country on the Department of State watch list. Purdue is widely known for its global research and teaching projects and couldn't prevent faculty from traveling to so-called dangerous areas, particularly when some of those places are home to international personnel and students. The phone call I received from West Lafayette's International Programs office to check on me was reassuring. I apologized for failing to let them know I had changed my flight.

Encounters with colleagues that struck me most were with two Chinese professors. The first, with George, was especially warming. George is kind and excitable, and at that time headed up our research office. A professor of economic history, he liked all things international, and had solicited my participation on a number of projects involving faculty and students. The summer before, I had traveled to Hong Kong on a collaborative research and teaching trip led by him. He was tireless and enthusiastic every moment, full of insight and anecdotes. He helped me come to appreciate history even more than I had, if that were possible, through his personal accounts of his vocational calling to the discipline.

George grew up during the Cultural Revolution, when intellectual pursuits in areas as truth-telling as history had become taboo, even punishable. When he reached college age, the widespread attacks on academics had come to an end, and he let his parents know his love for history had driven him to choose it as a major. They were crushed and fearful, having witnessed the government's attacks on historians through adult eyes. Nonetheless, he became a historian.

Our travels to and through Hong Kong allowed time for more conversations and the historical differences between the former British colony and the mainland became crystallized. I had visited Beijing, Shanghai, Harbin, Dalian, and other major cities in northeast China during a student recruiting trip in previous months. In comparing the two regions, one of the things I found most apparent was that Hong Kong was more, in a word, orderly. British rule had infused an unparalleled sense of formality there, and its experiences as a financial capital of the world had brought it a seasoned modernity that could not yet have developed in the rest of China, where growth was recent, fierce, and rampant. Still, some cultural similarities remained.

As we spoke of *feng shui* and the positive, healthy flow of energy on a day trip to the harbor, he pointed to a new high-rise apartment structure built on the side of a steep hill.

"Can you see how it is designed?" he asked us. There was a separation between the towers.

"Was it done that way for a reason?" another professor asked.

"According to the legend, the mountain is home to a dragon, which would be very angry if his view of the harbor were obstructed in some way. The architect was instructed to leave a space for the dragon."

The co-existence of modern and traditional beliefs in Asian society was intriguing and attractive to me. After learning more about *feng shui*, I placed a couple of red items strategically in my office for luck and gathered all of the foreign currency I had collected over the years, put it in an elaborate pencil holder I received as a gift in Shanghai. I then set them on the window ledge, in my prosperity corner. I cannot say that it worked; in fact, I might argue based on actual life circumstances that it did not. At least not the prosperity bit. But how is prosperity measured anyway?

When I ran into George just a couple days after the earthquake, he quickly reached out to grab my arm.

"I am so happy to see you!" I could do nothing but grin, as tears began to well up in my eyes.

"You are so lucky!"

I nodded.

"No, really. In Chinese custom we acknowledge something like this as being very lucky. You escaped an earthquake. It is a sign that you are a lucky person." He held my arm tighter. "A very lucky person."

"Why do you say that?" I did feel fortunate, but he introduced a whole new dimension to my understanding of luck.

"You should buy a lottery ticket!"

I laughed.

"No, it's true. This is a lucky time for you, a lucky person. Do it today."

"Okay, okay." I thought about it, but did not do it.

The next day, in the same spot, I passed another Chinese professor. Chen had headed up two of our engineering departments, and was equally energetic and engaging.

"Kathy! You are here!"

I nodded.

"I heard you were in Haiti but missed the earthquake. You are very lucky. A very lucky person."

"I guess so. I'm just happy to be back."

"You should buy a lottery ticket. This is a lucky time for you."

That evening on my way home, I needed to stop for gas. While I could have paid at the pump and been on my way, I decided to run in for a bottle of water. Above the cashier dangled dozens of rolled strips of lottery tickets.

"You want one?" he asked, perhaps concerned I might be holding up the line.

"What's a good one?"

"If I knew that, I'd be rich."

"How can I win the most money?"

"Powerball." I wasn't sure how that worked, but understood the drawing would not take place until the weekend. My lucky time might be running out.

"Nah. I should do something instant. Give me two of that kind." One on George's advice, I thought, and one on Chen's. I chose the prettiest ones displayed. He rolled his eyes, tore two tickets from above him, and handed them to me.

"This and the water? Six dollars and sixty-two cents."

I took my purchases, and stood aside while he waited on the others. I wanted to choose a space rather sacred, or in some way memorable, where scratching two tickets would change my life forever. There was a half-empty shelf next to some dusty STP. I took a nickel from my jacket pocket and did what I had to do. And there it was. I won two dollars and two free lottery tickets.

Communication with Haiti was chillingly limited but I learned a few days later that Hospice St. Joseph had collapsed.

33
Normal

The idea of starting classes was terrifying. I had been teaching for more than 20 years, but this time I did not know how I could possibly get up in front of a room full of students and go on with my lectures as usual.

In the days before students were to arrive I visited each of my rooms, practicing walking in and going through the motions required of the first few minutes of the first day. I placed my books in front of me – books I had used before – opened them, and touched the pages. They may as well have been blank. I looked up at the empty seats and opened my mouth and uttered a few sounds, as if to make sure my voice would work.

Before returning to my office, I visited the campus Counseling Center. The student manning the front desk watched me intently as I tried to make sense of what was wrong.

"I was in Haiti on the day of the earthquake and I don't seem to be coping with it very well. Not as well as I should be."

"Would you like to make an appointment to see someone on Monday?" he asked.

"No, classes are starting. That's ok. It's just that right now I can't imagine getting in front of my students without crying. Maybe I'll feel better in a couple days. That's ok," I said as I turned to go.

"Wait a minute," he said and disappeared into a back office.

My eyes were filled with tears. This trip was supposed to make me feel better about my job – about life – and it had done the opposite. He returned quickly.

"Maybe I will make an appointment," I told him.

"I can see you now," he replied.

He seemed to be a graduate student in the counseling program, or maybe he just looked young. It didn't matter. I just needed someone to talk to and he listened.

When I finally did teach, the presence of Haiti and all of its problems hovering over the classroom was not a problem. Rather, the fact that so many of my students seemed oblivious to it was what bothered me. When students repeatedly missed class, came in late, or failed to do the readings or turn in assignments I wanted so much to remind them that this would not happen in Haiti. There students walked miles to school and saw education as a privilege they would never dream of denying themselves. But I could not do that to them. They were raised in a society where education a given, and it was understandable that they took it for granted. I needed to recognize that their attitudes had not changed since before my trip. Mine had.

In early February, students from the honor societies in both history and political science asked if I would make a campus presentation about my trip there and what I had hoped for Haiti's future. I agreed and was stunned that the group in attendance filled the large lecture hall. I did my best to incorporate what I had learned about education with what the country's needs were following the earthquake. School development kept coming to mind so it played a significant role in what I said. It also helped me to reconcile Haiti's past with its future because education is a constant that links generations. One our best students approached me after the talk.

"Professor Tobin, you spoke a lot about developing education there but don't you think they have more immediate needs?" he asked.

"Yes," I replied. They did. But we were both right. Urgent relief efforts were still underway, but to think again of Haiti only in the short term would ignore its potential for years to come.

34
Thirst

Water is life. In the Great Lakes region we have a unique understanding of this. We know it to be true, but we take water for granted. When stopping for a moment to think about it – really think about it – we realize that water come to us with abundance, even majesty, to immerse ourselves in it, to bathe and shower, and splash in it. We water our lawns, irrigate our crops, and wash our cars with it. We watch our children run through it, dancing in the sprinkler spray, reaching for rainbows created by the sun's rays, wishing our adult maturity did not prevent us from doing it, too.

These images, these tactile sensations, these experiences exist wherever there is water. What makes it different for Great Lakers is that our water is fresh. Our water is drinkable. Our water can sustain human life at its very core. And our water seems unbounded in volume. In many other parts of the world water is comparatively scarce.

When visiting Haiti, at least beyond the hotels and restaurants where gracious hosts emphasize guest comfort, the dearness of water becomes more immediately evident. Ingrained with the warning, 'Don't drink the water,' visitors to the developing world are confronted with just what that means upon being shown their living quarters. Having spent a good part of the day getting to one's destination, thirst becomes inevitable. The more savvy traveler may have packed bottled water for the day, or remembered to ask the flight attendant not for soft drinks or coffee but for two cups of water at each opportunity. The more well-off traveler may have thought to purchase some four-, five-, or six-dollar bottle of water at the airport. But for many, getting the key to the room means dropping luggage, testing the bed, checking the view, and heading to the bathroom to freshen up. The dustiness of air and environment, or the exhaust and indescribable organisms that hang in the humid air of the topics compel the average U.S. traveler to wash.

The sensitive take notice of the very basic faucets and the trickle of water that flows from them, perhaps missing the water at home. A wash of the hands lathered with Dial – or whatever has been provided – and a splash of the face are in order. Just a splash. But fears creep in. What if some tap water were to accidently enter the mouth? What amount is needed to cause illness? A teaspoon? A few drops? And what illness? One that causes uncontrolled purging and certain death? What if it weren't swallowed? What if it were just a splash on the lips? All of this worry over something that should give life. Over something that is needed to sustain life.

In successfully brushing one's teeth, an American traveler crosses a threshold to survival. Removing the toothbrush from the perfectly zipped plastic bag, wondering if one can work quickly enough to prevent any airborne such and such from landing on the bristles. Uncapping a bottle of water destined to last through the remainder of the day. Pouring ever so little on the bristles just to moisten them, and then perhaps just a little more. Carefully set the bottle on the ledge of the small sink, circa 1945 to 1955, or perhaps for the more daring on the toilet tank, no on the rim of the shower stall. Then dotting the bristles with toothpaste thoughtfully selected from one hundred or more options at one's neighborhood mega-drugstore back home just yesterday. Then dotting it once more and wondering if one more splash of water might be in order. But more toothpaste would mean more rinsing, both of the mouth and the brush. Less toothpaste, less water. Brushing itself becomes a more heightened experience without the water running and morning news radio prepping one for the day. Perhaps there are street noises, perhaps there are country noises, but in either case, they are foreign. And the bristles wipe the teeth and the tongue, and there is just enough water to rinse the brush, the lips and the fingers that must gently reseal things away from anything airborne and keep thirst quenched for the remainder of the day.

In taking note of accommodations and surroundings, it is likely one will notice a pitcher of purified water and drinking glass on the dresser. Haitian hospitality and thoughtfulness provide an endless supply. Having watched women and children carry supplies of water, I became much more aware of my consumption. Judging the level of water remaining in the pitcher during the mid-afternoon measured against my thirst level or potential for thirst became nearly obsessive. And still, the supply was limitless.

On my last full day in Port-au-Prince, I took my empty pitcher to the second floor kitchen area, where a five-gallon container balanced in its frame, ready to be tilted for replenishment. But the jug was nearly empty. I tipped it carefully; its lightness making it more difficult to maneuver did not quite fill my pitcher halfway. I chose to leave some behind. While it teetered in my hand, I wondered why I hesitated – I, the Great Laker who seemed to waste water with abandon. But in Haiti, it becomes customary to take only what one needs. And for me, it became customary to consciously measure my thirst.

In trying to keep up just enough on the tragic news developments following the earthquake, I read the story of a woman and her daughter who were trapped on top of one another under the rubble of their home. The daughter, a 20-year-old who I pictured not unlike my own daughter, had all but given up hope. Her mother encouraged her to hold on, promising that they would be rescued. As the days wore on, she remained painfully aware of her daughter's incapacitating thirst, and maneuvered carefully to urinate into her hand and offer it to her so that she might survive. Though the act kept her alive for some time the daughter eventually died. The mother was rescued on the fifth day.

Her story touched me on so many levels. The desperation of trying to keep one's child alive under those circumstances was unimaginable to me. The idea of trying to survive that kind of thirst was … well, I just could not fathom that kind of thirst. The picture of both of them trapped was painted so vividly that images of others so trapped came into sharper focus. Trapped. I called Katie to tell her the story. I wanted to think I could do the same for her, and I prayed never to be in a position to do so. But how could I talk to my daughter about something like that? If there were some way to shelter her from any such ideas, I would. God, I missed her. When she answered, I spoke of mundane things, and eventually brought up the story of the woman and her daughter. And then I cried. She cried, too.

35
Promises

After my return, months went by before Christine and I could pin down a presentation date. We emailed briefly early on, acknowledging the earthquake. The substance of my talk would shift dramatically and we both wanted some time to pass in order to let things settle into more familiar rhythms, if that were possible. The entire country had become so intent on raising money for relief that it would be difficult to contextualize school and education matters in a way that transcended or disregarded the topic of money. I had promised this would be for information only.

We finally chose a day in May. She booked a room at Innsbrook Country Club and a strong sense of anticipation set in. I did have so much to share and I could not ignore the fact that I had strong family ties to the ground on which Innsbrook lay. Both my grandmother and father were born in houses that bordered the property there. The land had once been part of my great grandfather's farm. I had driven past many times, but never got out of the car to let my feet touch the earth. I knew being there would hold additional meaning for me.

Sadly, the presentation would not take place. Just hours before, my father fell gravely ill with an acute case of pneumonia. There was a chance he might not make it through the night. He had been ill for some time, battling the effects of diabetes and bouts of illness following a stroke. But that day things had taken a turn and his cough was relentless. Already in a weakened state, he seemed especially fragile. My mother and I conversed with him the best we could and then with each other, and we finally let him know we thought it best that he go to the hospital.

"Dad, we're going to call an ambulance," I told him.

He seemed relieved. He had been a strong, reliable, 1950s type of father and it was difficult for him to yield power and decision-making responsibility over the past few years. He had become physically incapacitated and mentally changed. As the eldest, and a daughter, I had had my share of clashes with him before I matured into young adulthood. He was an admirable family man who chose a decent way of life, coming home from work at 5:00 on the dot and tending to his garden when the weather was good. Above all, he was a man we could rely on.

Over the past many months, his body had become thin and stiff. He ate less and less and moved with increasing difficulty. It had been just a few weeks since we helped him to his last trip up the stairs, to stay in what used to be the "girls' room". My sisters and I helped our mother lift him from the bed to the chair and back again. It was the least we could do. I don't know how she managed.

Within a short time at the hospital, Dad was taken to the Intensive Care Unit. It was a solemn place. It saddened me to see so many patients there alone. I walked into the hallway and stared out the window. The ticking of time was palpable. I knew I had to phone Christine and back out. Remembering innumerable excuses from my students on test days and assignment due dates, I wondered if she would understand, if she would believe me. I did not know if this was truly the end, or just a close call. We had waited four months for the talk on Haiti, and I owed her a presentation. I could be back in three hours, I told myself. But I looked into the faces of my sisters, and knew I couldn't leave. My brother was on his way from Wisconsin.

"No, it's all right. Really." Christine sounded convincing, but my perception was skewed. "Listen, you need to be with your father."

Once again, I stared out the window. Community Hospital was just a half block from my parents' house, the house where I grew up. It was a neighborhood fixture, and from my 5th floor view, I could envision us running around the blocks as children, sometimes tying jump ropes to our bicycles and pulling our friends on roller skates. The area was nothing but a cornfield when my dad bought the lot, and he contracted the construction himself. Next to his family and garden, that house meant everything to him.

"Dad, I need to go talk to some people about Haiti," I wanted to say to him. "I'll be right back. I promise." I knew he would understand. But I couldn't bring myself to go. "Dad, you were the first person to teach me about Haiti," I whispered.

My dad was stationed in the Caribbean while in the Navy. He joked that when the Korean War broke out he was called back to the Great Lakes Naval Base to defend Chicago. But he must have spent enough time in the islands to make an impact on him. He never seemed much for souvenirs, but I remember handkerchiefs and painted pins with pictures of palm trees and sunlight. Some of my first memories were of looking through his boxes and wondering what kinds of places were home to such unusual things. There were photographs of him with other sailors standing near gigantic ships. The images were in black and white, but every time I saw a film about the Navy, I pictured him in living color, surrounded by blue skies and water. There was something about this Jamaica and Cuba and Haiti that lingered in his memory, and I was convinced my decision to study the Caribbean was influenced by that.

My thoughts turned to Innsbrook and a missed opportunity to be near the house where he was brought into the world at the same time he was so close to leaving it. I hoped to be there one day, but then again I also hoped he would live forever.

Dad lived a few weeks longer and died at home in hospice care. The sun shone on his funeral and he was buried at Calumet Park cemetery just south of the house where he was born. The cemetery property, too, was once part of his grandfather's farm. The funeral director was a family friend, and had arranged for a military commemoration. As the bugler played "Taps" I gazed at the men in the sailors' uniforms. They seemed so very young.

36
UNOGA

Renate and I stayed in close contact. The experience of being in Haiti at such a crucial time and then separated from the disaster made us feel powerless but brought us together. She was able to return a few months later and reported back whatever she could find out. Having spent so much time there, she had very close friends she needed to check on and had a good sense of what tangible steps might be taken that could help in long term development. After a good deal of thought, she told me about an idea for expanding the Université de la Nouvelle Grand'Anse through Haitian Connection, and organization she had developed to coordinate projects in the area.

UNOGA was situated far from the capital, and while it offered programs only in agronomy and management at a technical school level, the facilities were solid and the campus worth developing. Expanding offerings there that were improved with a foundation of one year of general studies could help raise the school to university status. It could also provide opportunities to surviving students who were displaced by the earthquake. And with adequate growth and sustainability it could help in regional development of the Grand'Anse. While Haitian university faculty might not yet be available, she said we could work to staff the first year program with U.S. and

European faculty who could teach in any of the social sciences, humanities, physical and biological sciences, and mathematics. We could also offer continuous instruction in languages and computer technology. By scheduling the courses in 3-week modules, students could experience intensive immersion in one subject at a time and faculty could volunteer their time without neglecting their classes back home. The idea sounded feasible and exciting and, knowing Renate, she could make it happen. I agreed to teach a course and offered to spread the word to other faculty who were interested. In a short time, we had commitments from professors in a wide variety of areas.

Creating a syllabus was a daunting task, though I kept telling myself it need not be. They were just students, after all, and I would be their professor. And this was a history course. I had taught history for years. Enough said. However, there were clearly new challenges here. First, the curriculum needed to be condensed into a three-week module. This was not impossible. As a graduate student I completed summer courses at the University of Chicago, which lasted only three weeks. Yes, they were intense, but I still remember much of what I learned. And in Haiti I would have them for longer periods of the day. Second, their English skills were minimal. There would be an interpreter, but that at least doubled the time it would take to get the information across in lecture, or cut in half the amount of material I could cover.

Also, it was difficult to determine what level of preparation they had. Because I had met with social studies teachers on my previous trip I had some idea of what was taught in middle school and high school. I knew they were accustomed to lectures, and that put my mind at ease. But I still was not sure just how much they knew about history and what nuanced understanding they would bring to class.

To a large degree this was more of a problem on my part, as the perspective I bring to my lectures was increasingly lost on students. Much of it has to do with the level of knowledge I have gained over the years, but it is compounded with the generational gap between me and my students that continues to grow wider. Common references to pop culture or current events I use at home might return puzzled looks. In Haiti they might be misunderstood even more.

Then there was the mystery of the classroom space. When at all possible, I visit my classrooms sometime before the semester begins, in order to get a feel for the rooms and to envision myself teaching there. No matter how many descriptions I had heard about the facilities at the Université de la Nouvelle Grand'Anse, I knew it would be unlike any I had ever worked in. On my previous visit with Renate and Corinne I had not set foot in the classroom buildings.

Putting the materials together posed a challenge as well. Successful learning of history relies on substantial reading and writing and it takes time to digest. Knowing that their skills in French were better than those in English, I searched for reading materials in French and I named the course *Histoire de l'Atlantique*. My intention was to look at the Atlantic world as a cohesive unit that has shared a common history through interaction of incredibly diverse cultures from Europe, Africa, and the Americas. I was able to find book chapters and articles that addressed native cultures, colonization, slavery, sugar and the development of Haiti, missionaries in the Caribbean, commercial competition between the French and Spanish, economic-based Caribbean wars between the French and British, and the American Revolution and its address of abolition. The reading demands may have seemed excessive, but I was careful to limit the number of pages required. I agree the concepts were huge, but hat is often the case in introductory history courses. There is just so much to cover.

As with my American students, even if they cannot read or grasp everything, it is essential for them to know what is out there, to know just how big the field is. This way, the more educated one gets the more likely they are to realize how little they know. That is not necessarily a bad thing. True education should foster a sense of confidence, but also humility. I do not want any students to feel overwhelmed to the point that they give up trying; rather, I want them to realize there is always more out there. Always more to learn. This is no more or less than I expect of myself.

I was advised to send a pdf file of the reading packet in advance so that someone from the school, or the students themselves, could print it out. As much as I hate to admit it, I did not trust the system to accomplish this. It was not that I didn't trust the school administrators or the students to do it. But knowing what I know about Haiti and its limits in technology, electricity and paper, I didn't want to put that burden on them. I would do it myself.

There was a lesson learned here. They could have done it themselves. As the first day of classes neared, enrollment soared, and I found myself attempting to reproduce more than 100 reading packets. My department photocopy machine was of little use. I resorted to paying for copies at a local office supply chain store. I signed up for every kind of deal in order to save the largest percentage, as this was suddenly costing hundreds of dollars. I even think I am now a member of some kind of "copy club" as I receive e-mail announcements from them still.

An even bigger challenge, however, was getting them there. I packed and repacked my suitcases, losing sleep the night before my trip and making difficult choices about what to leave behind. One of the instructors in our campus English as a Second Language program had been kind enough to donate boxes of textbooks and instructor's manuals for UNOGA, but I found it impossible to take more than a dozen or so. Books and anything like reading packets are tremendously heavy. Even though airlines had relaxed their baggage restrictions since the earthquake, allowing relief workers to take multiple suitcases filled with supplies at no extra cost, I was traveling alone and did not know how I could possibly maneuver with everything I wanted to take. This was one time when I could have kept things simple, but I have no regrets in asking them to read what I had decided on. Their dedication was excellent and their responses satisfying, at least for the most part. They were college students after all.

Knowing I would be physically in the classroom for only the middle week of the three scheduled for this module, I sent a list of essay questions ahead. There were two professors from other universities teaching modules in economics and English before I was to arrive, so I knew the questions could be distributed to the students easily. I kept the questions brief yet broad, allowing for a wide range of responses. I was not sure what to expect, but wanted to stimulate historical thinking before I arrived. I was happy my course fell comparatively early in the academic year – in late September to early October. History ideally should fall early in one's studies, as it sets the stage for everything else. Historians tend to think literally and chronologically, and perhaps I give my field far more worth than it deserves. Still, it is good to start with first things first.

These are the questions sent ahead:

-- Why do we study history?

-- How do historians and students find out what has

happened in the past?

--Why do you think it might be important to study Atlantic history?

I believed they were universal and answerable. I added, "You may meet with other students to discuss these questions in groups before you write your essays. They will be due on Monday, September 27."

It was my hope that they would take time to meet with their classmates to talk about history. Haitian culture is known for the value it places on relationships, and I believed that their existing relationships would facilitate this exercise as much as the exercise could help build future relationships. I have no way of knowing whether this worked or what impact it might have had, but I knew it was worth a try. College matriculation can be daunting, and fostering relationships early on can help with success. This concept is now something that gets a good deal of attention by university administrators and influencers of budgeting forces in the United States. It seems common sense to me, something I believed would transcend borders and work even better in a place like Haiti.

In asking the questions, I did not expect to get any specific responses. There were clearly no right or wrong answers. I looked forward to reading what they had to say.

37
Going Back

Arriving in Miami and waiting for my flight to Port-au-Prince, I imagined moving backwards in time. Leaving O'Hare had been uneventful but as I sat at Miami International thoughts of pre-earthquake hours returned. I remembered reminiscing about the morning sunlight shining on the children going to school and the sense of hope that seemed to permeate the country. I remembered my unexpected and intense thoughts of an estranged friend who I hoped would someday contact me and who did send an e-mail immediately following the earthquake. I remembered eating *arroz imperial* at the Cuban café near my gate. I fantasized about turning back the clock so that once I left Miami and my flight landed in Port-au-Prince everything would be as it was the last time I saw it.

But it was not. The huge crack in the wall of the airport terminal was the first sign. A driver picked me up and took me to an apartment which belonged to UNOGA's rector. I rode in silence. This was some ten months later and still rubble stood all around. The roads had been cleared but debris was piled nearby. People went on with their lives. In that respect Port-au-Prince seemed the same. Life had been hard before the earthquake, yet people went on with their lives. But my last memories included faces marked with hope, and those were missing. Perseverance was there, and fortitude, but so was a measure of gravity.

The apartment was substantial – large rooms tiled in marble, a wonderful shower, and an offer of dinner. Still, I felt very alone. There is less warmth and a certain degree of detachment in any major city, but as night began to fall, uneasiness permeated the neighborhood. I heard a gunshot in the distance – likely, I was later told, an indication of political violence surrounding the upcoming election. I had noticed the campaign posters throughout the city but was unable to gain much of anything from them except who seemed to have more publicity resources. I looked forward to the rural setting of UNOGA.

On my flight into Jeremie I met some nuns from Ohio, just outside Toledo. I like sisters. I told them I attended Catholic school for eight years and later a Catholic college, not to score points but to let them know in some way that I got it. I'm not sure what non-Catholics think when they see nuns – probably all kinds of things. Though becoming much less of a practicing Catholic, I still admired what they did. They are the backbone of the Church. First, they get things done, as in any patriarchal organization where the dominating males believe their positions, titles, and sitting around the table having meeting after meeting are what matters. If it were not for the women of the operation, not everything would get done and that is true for the Catholic Church, as well.

And I like talking to sisters. They're interesting and often funnier than one might imagine. They tend to do noble things and are pretty fearless. I once visited an incredibly beautiful convent in Antigua, Guatemala, where the nuns lived in absolute simplicity and took vows of silence. Each had a room of her own with a small bed and desk. The gardens there were among the most perfect I had ever seen, and I wanted to live there, too. There is nothing like being on one's hands and knees, digging in the dirt, in order to help something miraculous and magnificent grow. Spending the rest of my days protected from the noise of the outside world seemed very appealing at the time. I still had kids at home and averaged a hundred students each semester, which undoubtedly added to the attraction of this alternative lifestyle. It was so peaceful. My Spanish was fine, especially my reading. My conversation skills were weaker, but the vow of silence would make things all the easier.

Not many nuns live like that. Most are out in the world doing good work and sometimes, as in the case of these sisters, that takes them to places like Haiti. I liked hearing about their travel. I also liked that they had brought along a young female college student. I looked at her, trying to figure out if perhaps she was considering the sisterhood, or that she was just very Catholic. There is something calming about being around people who are called to that life. And perhaps because I had been raised Catholic, it did not seem so strange to me at all.

After a conversation that took up most of the hour-long flight, we arrived in Jeremie, stepped off the plane, and waited for our bags. After many minutes of growing confusion, it became clear that most of our bags had not made it onto the plane. There was a good deal more supplies – medicine and such – that making their way into post-earthquake Haiti and on small planes the weight limits prohibited transport of everything we would like to bring directly with us. It was unclear who decided what made it or not or how that decision was made. With some extra attention, pleading and/or clout, all of one's packages might make it. Evidently neither the sisters nor I had done what we might have, and our belongings were left in Port-au-Prince, at least until the next day's flight.

It was an inconvenience for me, but it was only Saturday and my class did not begin until Monday. I was a bit upset with myself for having become lax with my things. After having my bag lost in Port-au-Prince in January, I was careful to divide my clothing and teaching materials between two suitcases, having enough in my carry-on to get by. But once in Port-au-Prince, I felt relieved, and assumed I could check both of them with confidence. I was wrong. Huge cardboard boxes holding some sort of provisions seemed to take precedence, and both my bags were left behind. It might take an extra trip to the Tortug'Air office in the morning to retrieve them, and I was promised they would arrive next day. I would survive. However, I knew it would be an inconvenience for my hosts.

I'm not sure what the sisters had been transporting, but one of them did not take the news of the delay lightly. She found the baggage handlers and really let them have it. It reminded me of the experiences of grade school with the stricter nuns and was a sight to behold.

As for my things, I was right and there were no worries.

38
TEACHERS' HOUSE

The house designated for teachers in the UNOGA program was inviting. The property drive was enveloped in trees and I did not seem to mind that much of the vegetation could use a good pruning. I'm not sure what it is about the need for pruning that catches my attention. I tend not to notice people's dust, piles of papers, or even dirty dishes. But I notice when a lilac bush could use a good lopping. Perhaps it is related to the fact that I get little satisfaction from housework but the unspoken rewards of yard work seem endless to me. I can do it for hours on end. That and ironing. I make no judgment about the need for someone's clothing to be ironed; in fact, I prefer the freedom of wearing wrinkled cottons and linens myself. However, the act of ironing brings me tremendous gratification. Not so much in the vision of a neatly hanging wardrobe at its conclusion, but in the very action of pressing out imperfections with a bit of heat and steam. I imagine pressing out the imperfections of life with each glide. It helps to watch classic romantic comedies while I do it. The characters always find ways to work their ways through the stickiest of situations. Imperfections seem to be ironed out in those scripts.

It was not my place to spend any time pruning while in Haiti. After all, I had students to meet, readings to outline, and lectures to prepare. But I did fantasize making a return trip one day to neaten up the yard. I also wanted to see the house painted, but was in no way interested in doing that myself. The structure was wooden and painted many times over, a light gray-blue with bright aqua-green trim. It had been owned by the mother of the university's director, I understand, and must have been a century or more old. Its porch swept the entire back and side of the house – a veranda framing glorious living quarters of days gone by. It reminded me of my grandmother's porch, far simpler but with trim painted Kelly green many times over, a cultural curiosity brought from Ireland by my grandfather I was told. More so, the rocker invoked childhood memories of creaking wood runners pressing against the slats beneath me. Back and forth, back and forth, arm rests so wide the span of my hand could not yet air reach. During late afternoons following classes I found the rocker soothing – with my head resting back, warm, aromatic air filled my senses. On the first day the fragrance struck me as unfamiliar – not the hydrangeas or lilies of the valley I knew so well. But I kept my eyes closed, half dreaming and half knowing I was in Jeremie and not northwest Indiana. My hands reached the width of the arm rest, and then some. For just a moment I wanted to be a child again, and not a grown woman in a foreign culture with work to do.

The hours spent on the porch deep in thought allowed for more time to consider the seriousness of deforestation in other parts of the country. Around me dangled fruit and flowers, making it difficult to remember the erosion-marked hillsides I had crossed near Fort Liberté several years before. I empathized with the women who opted to use charcoal for fuel and wondered why the impact had not been so great here. Burning cut trees into charcoal to in turn burn for cooking has been criticized as a short-sighted use of natural resources and the behavior characterized Haitians as desperate and ignorant. But like every other human being on earth, Haitians need to eat. And unless they are willing to eat only raw food, they need fuel for cooking. Neither the cities nor the rural areas are equipped to supply sufficient electricity or natural gas – the energy much of the developed world depends upon for use by the general population. At least not yet.

Many non-Haitians have recommended solar ovens, and producers have actively marketed there. Some have solicited donations from very well-intentioned in order to increase the supply there. But there are two major drawbacks to solar ovens in Haiti. First, using them requires a change in custom, a change in habit. Yes, that may seem like a minor drawback, but the thought of even switching from gas to electric cooking, or vice versa, makes many of us cringe. I have known people who cooked for years on electric stoves and would not dream of cooking with gas. When I switched from gas to electric, I did so with trepidation and only because I got married and moved into my husband's apartment. It had an intimidating, though very cool late-70s/early 80s harvest gold, electric stove. My mother had cooked with gas, and her mother. I burned endless dinners – and breakfasts and lunches – because I could not turn the heat down fast enough.

From there we bought our first house, with a gas stove. From there a bigger house, with a top of the line electric, which I ultimately had replaced with gas when we remodeled the kitchen. Cooking with gas was just plain easier for me. Easy on, easy off. Quick high heat, quick low heat. Such is the life of the American woman. We have options, and we generally base our choices not on what is best for the environment or the general economy, or the long-term development of the country. So expecting Haitian women to do so under much more dire circumstances is something we should more carefully assess. Plus, cooking over charcoal versus cooking with the sun is far more different than switching from gas to electric.

Second, as sunny as Haiti can be it is not always that way. In fact, it can rain for days on end. To depend on the sun for the family's daily nourishment on a consistent basis, is unrealistic. In addition, even on sunny days, the people of Port-au-Prince would not necessarily have access to the sun. Housed very closely together, they would be stepping over each other's solar ovens placed in any sun visible between concrete block structures for even part of the day. A few might be placed on rooftops, but that is not practical either. Perhaps a few toward the street, but they lie close to the ground, and placing them anywhere near walkways or roads puts the food too close to standing water and sewage. For now, at least, cooking over charcoal is the answer for most.

Sitting on the porch of the teachers' house, I realized that if this were all I had seen of Haiti, I might never have taken the concerns of deforestation seriously. There appeared to be more than enough food-bearing plants to sustain the population. Local leaders affiliated with the Ministry of Agriculture acknowledged the abundance with respect and noted its vulnerability. There were no substantive laws protecting the trees and Haitians could not be blamed for cutting them for fuel out of tradition and desperation. The impact of such practices might not be readily apparent, but it was there. And once the road to Port-au-Prince was completed, the effects might be drastic. Planners had hoped trucking produce to the capital would be more economically sound than losing investments through shipping that resulted in significant spoilage. Conservationists argued that no such promises should be made. Trucking, too, would result in spoilage, resulting in no greater profits. In addition, and more critically, the road could more easily allow for mass transport of cut trees for use in the most densely populated part of the country. For now, they promoted keeping them in place by teaching the value of what they produced while alive, primarily fruit.

After a breakfast of seemingly endless provisions of oranges, mango, pineapple, bananas, and some bread with butter and cheese, it felt a privilege to sit on the porch and wait for my ride to school. The porch was a perfect place to sit quietly in the morning as I waited for my ride to school. I had become very accustomed to driving myself everywhere back home – American suburban mom to the max. Being chauffeured made me feel at first a little uneasy but increasingly special. Each day, I eagerly took to the high-backed rocking chair, keeping one eye opened so as not to miss the driver's arrival.

The ride to UNOGA was just a few miles and 40 minutes long, with stops at various points in town and a winding drive along the dirt road to the school's entrance. I sat in the passenger's seat and conversed little with the driver, in part due to language difficulties but also because I wanted to capture every visual aspect and commit them to memory. Women trekked from the hills to market balancing large baskets of fruit on their heads. Children played in groups with whatever makeshift toys they could find. Men went about their business – repairing, washing, and producing whatever they could. Buildings needed paint and potholes needed fill. Animals walked the streets causing motor vehicles to veer. Shops welcomed visitors, their signs often untranslatable to me. I imagined what daily life was like for the hundreds of Haitians I saw each morning. Along the way we picked up students who eagerly jumped in the back of the truck.

"Good morning, Teacher!" each one shouted with school day smiles unknown in the U.S.

"Good morning," I replied, wishing my head were less filled with details of the coming day's lectures so I might remember their names. We also picked up Magalie, a school administrator who wore so many hats it was impossible to know her exact title or position.

Once on the rural road, the ride became quiet except for the occasional motor scooter whizzing by. It felt good to see the entrance to the campus, which was marked by a small gate. Once inside, it seemed little had changed from the time I was able to see the presentation by Renate and Corrine on mental health. The chicken coops were there, as were the areas devoted to agricultural experimentation and pig husbandry. The lush grassy areas reaching to the river and the classroom and administration buildings were there. But there was something added. Large canvass tents emblazoned with "UN" were situated near the garden. They were erected to house students who had arrived from outside Jeremie. The living quarters were not ideal, but this was a sign that word had spread of a new post-secondary educational opportunity. As I walked toward the assembly hall, students gathered on the grounds by the dozens.

39
CLASS

I love teaching. Preparing for and meeting each new class can be daunting but I still love teaching. My work at UNOGA was to be quite different, but my years of experience provided a sense of calm as I entered the assembly hall. Because of high enrollment the regular classrooms would not suffice. The energy permeating the space was invigorating.

There were far more students than expected, and the number grew each day I was there. Before my introduction, Magalie made announcements to the students regarding registration matters, tuition payments, completion of work from the previous module on economics, and the delivery of grades. Questions regarding my own assessment and evaluation design swirled in my head. I was advised that students expected rigor and a tough grading scale and I complied. That was clear in my syllabus. But I had not developed any sort of rubric to judge performance, for I honestly could not predict what they might be able to accomplish. Planning and flexibility were the best qualities I could bring to this situation. By the first day I became aware that the economics module had been exceptionally challenging for many of the students and part of me wanted to go easy on them. However, that was not an option.

As Magalie spoke, I surveyed the group. It was huge. A general headcount told me there were more than 120 students. Desks were lined in rows along the concrete floor, 15 to 20 deep. Daylight peered through the walls, making it easier to see the front half of the class. Magalie and I stood on a platform some 3 or 4 feet above the desks. They were not tiered in any way, so I plotted how I would walk up and down the aisles as I spoke to them about history, hoping to keep their attention. I was grateful for the opportunity to get my bearings. It did not take long for the sea of unfamiliar students to transform into a group of college-aged individuals, not so different from my students in Indiana. Eager, engaged ones sat in the front, raising their hands and responding immediately to what Magalie was saying. Others were half-listening and half-conversing with their classmates. Some appeared disengaged, some appeared tired. Some looked at us with extreme skepticism and it was a pleasant surprise once again to learn that those can be the best students of all. One quietly got my attention.

"Do you want our work?" he asked.

"Pardon me?"

"We answered the questions you gave us," he explained.

"Oh, yes, yes!" I responded quickly and they handed their papers toward the front. They did receive the questions I had posed and they did write out their answers. And here they were, passing them forward as any students would have in any of the many classes I had taught before. This was going to work just fine, I thought to myself.

Each day when giving my lectures, one young man in particular watched my every move with a very serious look on his face. He listened intently and seemed to question everything I said, not verbally but mentally. At least that is what I sensed. He put me on edge, though not in a bad way. It is essential that teachers attempt to be impeccable in their word. We are not perfect, but we should not be clever or careless in what we convey. While it is good to have students around who can joke a bit and keep things light, it is equally valuable to have at least one who serves as a reminder that investigating human history is serious business.

Nothing can compare to the teaching of Caribbean slavery, especially to students of African descent. That must sound so white of me. When I say teaching Caribbean slavery, by no means do I suggest a justification for such a practice, nor the perpetuation of memory with the intent to keep the image of black as slave alive. From time to time teaching has brought "out of body" experiences, allowing me to observe what is happening in the classroom space while I go about doing my job. It happened when I exchanged glances with the serious young man, and it happened as I looked out across the vastness of dark faces in front of me. In the past, my discussions of slave history invoked unique and personal reactions from my students of African descent. Here, all of my students were of African descent, and the story of slavery had shaped the entire country differently.

I once attended an anti-war demonstration where some marchers wore t-shirts printed with the message "Teach Peace," about which I very much agree. Others wore shirts stating "Stop Teaching War," about which I also very much agree. But upon engaging in conversation with one, I learned that they meant stop teaching about war, for in teaching about war, we were continuing to keep the image and possibility alive. In his view, the very introduction of real world examples served to indoctrinate youth and sustain a society's militaristic tendencies. But I could not imagine not teaching war. Nor could I imagine not teaching slavery, and it was so much a part of this Haiti course on Atlantic history.

After a few days, one student was emboldened enough to ask why the course was called "Atlantic History" and not just "History" for it seemed that that was what they were learning. Other students agreed. The comment made me realize how much their education had centered on the Atlantic story until this point, and I recalled the textbook examinations from my earlier trip. Though I did not have an opportunity to look in depth at the subject matter covered in each grade before one would enter college, what I did learn was that much attention focused on historical developments that ultimately shaped Haiti. I reminded them that there was much that took place in the world outside of the Atlantic, making casual references to early advancements in places such as Mesopotamia and China. They agreed. The comment also made me more aware of just how much I was asking of them in such a short amount of time. We were, in fact, covering a wide swath.

Adding to the challenge was the fact that I was teaching with an interpreter. Doing so naturally doubles the time necessary for lectures and question and answer sessions. The quality of interpreting varied, from dynamic early in the session to more static and limited later on. The interpreter with which I developed the best rapport was an English teacher from town named Antoine. His language skills were impeccable and he was comfortable in his interactions with students in a way that could be developed only from years in the classroom. However, he apologized repeatedly for not being able to do his best due to tremendous pain from a dental problem. I did not notice that his interpreting was hindered in any way, but could tell from the tension in his face as the day wore on that it must have been very difficult for him. He was unable to come in the following day.

"I need to pull my tooth," he said when I last saw him before he left. His manner of phrasing seemed strange, considering his English abilities. But I blamed it on the pain. Subsequent interpreters did just fine, but the class meetings did not flow in the same way.

Another challenge to moving swiftly through the material was the students' fascination with topics I covered early on, especially those relating to Native Americans. Experience has taught me to adhere as carefully as possible to a course calendar insuring we do not get too far behind. It is natural to want to devote more time to each aspect of history, but logistically demanding to cover hundreds of years in even fifteen weeks, let alone three. Students complain, for example – and rightly so – that professors rush through the post-Vietnam War era due to lack of time. At UNOGA I had my sights on laying the groundwork for Enlightenment influences on independence and abolition movements to be addressed at the end of the course, but the students could not seem to stop asking questions about the indigenous tribes of the Americas. I had introduced the subject briefly to demonstrate the cultural differences among inhabitants of the various continents before they encountered one another, expecting students to show more interest in the cultures of Africa and Western Europe. But as the discussions wore on I recalled how quickly the indigenous population disappeared from the Caribbean following the European conquest, resulting in an absence of indigenous influence on many of the islands. They wanted to learn as much as they could.

The video I brought seemed to feed their curiosity. I was told before my arrival that it would be possible to show videos to the class, which was a relief. Just as they served to bring the historical world to U.S. students in a more powerful way, I believed they could do the same for students who had far less exposure to the outside. The students themselves eagerly assisted in upending some tables and placing them aside one another on the raised area at the front of the room to function as the basis of a projection screen. Magalie brought some white bed sheets from home, which they draped over the tables and fastened with clips. They took special care to smooth any folds to make sure we had the best possible viewing surface. Watching them gave me a much better appreciation for the technology-ready classrooms to which I had become accustomed. Accentuating that appreciation was the effort it took to provide electricity for the projector. Students fired up the generator and made sure all the connections were in order. In an instant, others leapt to the platform and raced to the wall behind our makeshift screen.

"Is there a problem?" I asked.

"Problem?" one of the young women replied. She had recently moved to Jeremie from Cuba with her family. Her English was good and she took every opportunity to converse with me.

"Is there something wrong back there?"

"No," she said, laughing. "They're charging their cell phones. They heard the generator."

I found the cross-cultural attachment to cell phones amusing. Making-do while living in a country with scarce electricity made college students resourceful in their own special ways.

I also liked the fact that they wore blue jeans and t-shirts – more than one displaying a portrait of Barack Obama – and carried backpacks. Paper was scarce, but they brought what they could. And many were quick to show me that they had brought history books to class. Somehow, someway, somewhere, they had found old history textbooks and shoved them into their backpacks. The delight of having in hand a textbook that was not required but might supplement learning contrasted markedly from much of my experience in the U.S. I shook my head, beginning to realize just how much I would miss them.

40
Rain

When the rain was heavy, everything came to a stop. Four days into my class, I waited for my ride to school, which didn't come and didn't come. Micheline, the woman who cooked for me, assured the best she could that it would arrive when the skies cleared. I imagined how difficult it might be to transport the students who depended on us for a ride to sit on water-soaked benches in the back of the truck, while rain soaked their perfectly prepared school outfits. So it made sense to wait. And I waited. I wondered how I would be able to cover all the material expected for that day. The truck arrived when the rain finally stopped an hour or so later and, like clockwork, we picked up Magalie and the others along the way.

Maneuvering through town proved more difficult as the depths of potholes were more difficult to gauge. They were filled with water to their brims. Our travel time doubled. Once into the countryside, the mud had softened and become slick. Travel time tripled. My worries about original schedules and lessons planned subsided when I listened to the students joking and carrying on behind me. They were unfazed by the delay, and seemed happier than ever to be on their way to class. I imagined they would stay well into the late afternoon if I had asked them to.

Once we arrived, it appeared that the clouds might stay at bay, at least for a while. Class went on as usual. Students were eager and I was so grateful that the rain had subsided. The huge lecture space covered with a sheet metal roof could have become an echo chamber with the pelting of rain. I was told the level of sound in such classrooms found throughout Latin America can be deafening, making learning next to impossible.

I was happy to have a room at all. I was reminded of the collapsed university classrooms in Port-au-Prince, where many hundreds of students not unlike mine had been buried in earthquake rubble. In subsequent months, surviving students – particularly the younger ones – had been terrified of entering schools. The aftershocks were relentless, making matters worse. University students were fortunate to have classes continue in tents provided by various organizations, including the United Nations. Here, eight months following the earthquake, Port-au-Prince students were unable to experience a learning setting with which they were familiar. We had hoped to see more opportunities outside of the Port-au-Prince region, which is what prompted our investment in the Université de la Nouvelle Grand'Anse. Still, we could not possibly have handled any more students. By mid-week, enrollment in my class had grown to more than 140 and was still climbing.

Attendance was down a bit due to the rain that day. I had come to understand how common this is, especially in rural Haiti. Where students often travel an hour or two by foot to school rain-washed unpaved roads make the trip impossible. I had only been told this in the past. Now I could see the effects with my own eyes. Motor scooters can help, but not for elementary school children. So classes are often cancelled. This is the case during the rainy season of winter. Compounded with numerous holidays, holy days, feast days, and scheduled breaks, winter sessions are problematic. However, the sheer idea of students making hour or two treks to school on all days possible is tremendously hearting for a teacher. I knew those who missed would be there if they could.

I carried on class only until early afternoon so as not to risk students getting caught in a downpour on the way home. But just as class let out it began to rain again. I first ran to the administration building for a quick break and then across the grass to the building which housed the computers. I wanted to check my email and could hear the generator running. The students knew this had become my routine and had fueled the generator and fired it up. The "computer building" looked as if it had housed some classes in the past. Remnants of instructional tools hung on the walls, but the rooms were empty and the concrete floors were covered with dust. The light was good, however, and I pictured occupied desks one day, maybe 30 or so to each of the rooms. Perhaps there were desks there at one time that had been relocated to the assembly hall area as our enrollment grew.

Heavy, wooden stair steps – resembling a ladder with rungs – led to the second floor. It was not an easy climb, but I knew my e-mail waited at the top. There were offices there, and I was so grateful to anyone who would let me use their computer. The office space was tight and the few computers at hand were several years old, but they were precious. They were safer upstairs, should a hurricane sweep the area with flooding in its wake. Or perhaps they were located there when the first floor had been used for classes.

Checking e-mail took a little time, and I was never sure what to expect once I opened the door to my world back home. Day to day communication took on another dimension as it was sometimes difficult to relate to the U.S. culture I had left behind. Magalie worked busily at a desk across the room, calculating payments and writing out receipts for students who had just joined the class. Attempting to verify lists against my attendance sheets, her demeanor became more animated and her Creole more fascinating. I loved watching her work and imagined being able to understand what she was saying.

Keeping track of student enrollment can be challenging under any circumstances, but this situation seemed to bring on a new level of frustration. I recalled meeting her on my previous visit and she seemed so calm, collected, and charming. Her leadership and grace were remarkable. But now I got to see her at work. Hard at work. The administration had only recently decided on a small tuition requirement of every student and put in place a process where they could not receive their grades until it was paid. With rapid continuing growth, they were making quick decisions about when to stop taking students in. These were difficult calls to make, and I did not envy the position Magalie was in. I did admire her ability to end each day laughing. She clearly loved what she was doing, frustrations and all.

By this time in the week, the changes in climate and lifestyle were taking their toll on me. The Caribbean always does. Maybe it is the Irish in me, but I do look out of place there. Within days, my nose and forehead were sunburned and my hair was a mess of frizz. Makeup and contact lenses fell by the wayside and my attempts to dress with a sense of professionalism failed. Advertisements for Caribbean travel that depict women perfectly coiffed and clad in the latest sexy beachwear, looking lovely and graceful, their hair flowing in the gentle breezes, are so very different from my own real experiences. Even when my husband and I took the kids to Cancún for a week – where we had the luxury of hot showers and hair dryers – I felt endlessly caked with salt and sand. Don't get me wrong; the glories of allowing my body to become one with nature, to be changed by nature, are priceless. It's just that what emerges – at least in my case – is not something one would see highlighted in any marketing campaign.

On this trip I chose some rayon pants and short-sleeved linen shirts, thinking I could not go wrong. They held up fairly well, but were as plain as could be. And by this point in the week I had totally lost control of my hair. Totally. The bathing accommodations had made it impossible to wash my hair thoroughly. A five-gallon bucket of nippy rainwater was waiting for me each morning in the bathtub. Using a small pan to pour enough on my head to wet my hair and then more to prepare my body for a good soaping proved a startling beginning to each day, no matter how much I prepared mentally for it. I longed for a seemingly endless supply of hot water pouring from a modern, adjustable, massaging shower head. Perhaps I should have lived more fully in the moment, mindful that rainwater could indeed cleanse my hair sufficiently if I would just give it a chance, and grateful for the periodic precipitation that made the collection of water possible. Gratitude and acceptance miraculously allow nature to do its work. Resistance and grumbling do the opposite.

What I was left with was an air-dried thick, curly mop top – not short enough to be stylish, not long enough to be smoothly tied back. I had decided to go without washing it altogether for 2 days out of 3. Thursday's rain gave it an added dimension, allowing it to reach near afro stages. As I caught up on e-mails that day, I could see that life back on campus was going on as usual. My inbox was filled with meeting announcements, information on new administrative processes and procedures, and calls for conference paper proposals. An occasional inquiry from a friend wondering about life in Haiti required some kind of response, but it was difficult to find the words. Listening to the hum of the generator, I knew just how much effort it had taken to gain access to the internet at all, so I chose my words carefully.

"Things are going well. The students are great." That was about all I could say at that point.

A quick tap into Facebook allowed for a bit more levity.

"Lost control of my hair and am considering dreadlocks," I posted as my status. The "likes" and comments were immediate.

I wondered what my friends knew about this mysterious place. They wanted to know more, but time would not allow. Computer access was very limited and the internet slow. Still I was fascinated by the speed with which we could connect to the world beyond the Department of the Grand'Anse. As fascinating as it was watching pages download at a pace much slower than I was accustomed to back home, life moved almost in real time. The real time of the modern world.

UNOGA students had embraced everything that computers had to offer and used them whenever and wherever possible. But they were few. Students surfed the web whenever they had an opportunity – for school research and for pleasure – and typed their assignments and printed them for me. The majority had e-mail addresses, and many were on Facebook. Thanks to the support of donors abroad, internet cafes emerged using PCs and laptops that were no longer wanted. The infrastructure remained poor and downloading complex documents and photos seemed to take an eternity. There was no question that they could improve their situation with computer technology when given the opportunity. They were ready.

Still, the rhythm of life remained slow. After I finished

my internet communication with friends and colleagues, I descended the stairs and walked through the classroom to see a girl sitting on a metal folding chair, looking out the doorway. It was pouring rain. I stepped onto the porch and stuck my hand out, reaching beyond the roof line, to see just how heavy it was coming down. Then I zipped up my briefcase, held it close to my chest, and started down the steps.

"Where are you going?" the girl asked.

"I was just going to run over to see if there were any students in the library. They might have some questions about their papers."

"But it's raining."

"Yes." I looked at her and then out across the field. It could not have been more than fifty or sixty yards, but it became clear that my running to the library in the rain would be somehow unusual, or even inappropriate. I was not sure if that was because I was a woman or a teacher, or that I did not have an umbrella.

"Wait until it stops," she told me.

Another student came down from the offices upstairs, peered through the doorway, turned back to find another folding chair and sat nearby, looking out at the rain. They did not speak to one another. They just waited. I suddenly became conscious of some latent exasperation I apparently held. No wonder they can't get anything done in this country, I thought to myself. It's only rain, for God's sake. But I stopped short. I had come here to learn as well as teach, and this lay on a slippery slope from being an observer to being a condescending judge. So I found another chair and sat with them. Our language limitations added to the silence as the three of us sat.

The rain was beautiful, actually. It fell with a force, though not enough to pose a flooding risk. Rather, it pelted the ground, softening the carpet of grass. The larger vegetation seemed not just to withstand it but welcome it. The larger the leaf, the larger the reach, and the larger the surface with which to catch moisture. Droplets cascaded from each leaf to the one below, and flowers seemed to cup more attentively toward the sky. Though they were not within my view, I envisioned the fields planted to the side of the building grasping and storing whatever wetness came their way. I remembered my parents' garden and helping to water seedlings with a milk jug to see them on their way, taking a moment to sit between rows to watch drooping leaves rise and strengthen. Some of the most special times of my life took place with my father in that garden. He worked an accounting job at an oil refinery but seemed so at home alone, digging in the dirt. The infrequent rainstorms of Indiana's Julys were welcomed, for without them I wondered how it could be possible for the juice of each tomato or cucumber to form. I, too, had watched it rain on fields of green, but not in many years, before life got in the way. And I came to see this cultural difference not so much as one between the U.S. and Haiti, but between urban and rural life.

As the rain stopped, the others came down from upstairs and we walked together to the dining room for a very late lunch. The rhythm of eating differs in Haiti, for access to food is not as instantaneous. I was very hungry. My huge breakfast of fruit had held me until the end of class, but I had come to look forward to lunch on campus. It always consisted of a rice and beans dish, an array of fresh vegetables – usually including tomatoes and onions – and fish or some type of seasoned meat. Today it was chicken. Chicken was becoming more common in Haiti and they were raised as part of the agronomy program at UNOGA. A few generally wandered outside the area where the coop was located and near the assembly hall and dining room. As usual, the lunch was delicious, and topped off with sugary fruit-ade or glass-bottled Coca Cola with a straw made it an especially welcomed part of the day.

From there the return home was gloomy. Low-hanging heavy clouds continued threats of rain while moisture rose from the soaked ground. The students and Magalie had wiped dry the benches in the back of the truck but rode with less enthusiasm than usual. I leaned my head over my arm that rested on the window to capture the scent of the wet earth. The fragrance differed from that of days before and I smelled a hint of smoke. It reminded me of campfires on humid summer nights. The smoke did not pass as we neared Jeremie; rather, it seemed to grow stronger. Once at the teachers' house, I jumped down and said good-bye to the driver.

"*Mesi*! And see you tomorrow!" I said as I waved.

"Yes! See you tomorrow!" he replied.

The house seemed empty. Micheline must have delayed dinner preparations knowing the rain had extended our day. Too tired to make an immediate trip upstairs, I put down my books and papers and sat in the rocker on the porch. By that time the amount of smoke wafting through the neighborhood concerned me. The best way of knowing whether it should cause alarm was to judge by the reactions of the locals. Through the entrance to the driveway I could see women walking back up the hill with half-filled baskets of fruit, and men going about their usual activities. Children played games in the same ways they generally did. The smoke did not appear to worry them. Then I saw Antoine, the English teacher who had interpreted for me earlier in the week. He smiled, seemingly in less pain.

"Hello!" he said.

"Hi! How is your tooth?" I asked, getting up.

"Terrible but better," he said with a laugh. "Please, don't

get up." He sat down across from me.

"I suppose that is good news. I missed you in class. The interpreter who followed you could not compare." It was true. The man was nice enough and very helpful, but he seemed nervous and limited much of what he said to the students, making me wonder whether they were getting all of the information they needed.

"Thank you," he said, a little embarrassed. He sat back in his chair and proceeded to fill me in about his tooth.

"Wait," I interrupted. "I do want to hear about it, but first can you tell me why it is so smoky?" He did not seem concerned in the least.

"They are smoking out the mosquitoes," he said. "They do it after each heavy rain to prevent them from breeding."

"Ahh…" I nodded. "That makes sense. I guess. Does it work?"

"I am not sure. It is the custom." The air grew progressively worse as he showed me his tooth, or the space where his tooth had been.

"It's gone!"

"Yes, pulled."

"It must feel better."

"Yes. Now I must see a dentist." I did not hear much of what he said after that, though our conversation carried on for some time and covered a variety of topics. I could not help but wonder if he or a friend had pulled out his tooth, hoping to avoid a trip to the dentist altogether, or if it was customary to pull one's own teeth. I wish I would have asked.

"I have a lot to learn about Haiti," I told him.

"You will have to come back," he said.

"I would like that." It was my plan, but I knew that plans did not always work out.

41
MICHELINE

One day I arrived home after teaching to find my underthings hand-washed and hanging on the balcony rail. It was a bit of a surprise and a little disconcerting but Micheline was doing everything she could to make my stay perfect.

The proficiency level of her English paralleled that of my Creole, which meant both were pretty much next to nonexistent. But that did not stop us from communicating. We both said "thank you/*mesi*" a lot. What could be better than that? In the greater scheme of things, gratitude is what one should express more than anything. The universe, it is said, will not give us more of what we want or what we think we need unless we are truly grateful for what we have already been given. A sincere state of mind and heart will allow our energy to vibrate at a higher frequency, making us feel better and allowing us to attract more goodness into our lives. In any case, I was truly thankful for all that Micheline was doing, and that we at least had a common understanding of "thank you/*mesi*." Thinking back, I'm not sure why she was thanking me for anything. On the other hand, I had everything to be thankful for.

A few days into my stay at the house, I returned from long hours of teaching. Micheline appeared and greeted me with her wonderfully cheerful "*bonsoir*." She let me know that she had made something that sounded like "quiche" for dinner and on the table, there was something that looked like quiche. I knew it would be delicious, because everything she made was just that. Then she motioned with her hands and spoke of something that sounded like "culottes." From my mid-70s high school French class I vaguely remembered this meaning something different from the culottes that were fashionable then. Seeing that it would take me a while to make sense of what she was saying, Micheline took my arm and led me upstairs. I started toward my room, but she instead took me down the narrow hallway to a small balcony from which the Caribbean was visible in the distance. There all the panties I had worn thus far were gleaming in the late afternoon sun. And I had not even asked. As difficult as it is to live in Haiti, having one's bed made, meals prepared, and clothes washed can spoil a person. At that moment, the idea of taking her home with me flashed across my mind.

Micheline was more than gracious from the beginning of my stay. She even loaned me a dress to wear. It was a sleeveless, navy, rayon shift, tying at the back, with a medium print of lighter blue flowers. It was a perfect fit and far more comfortable than the slacks I had brought, which in advance seemed perfectly appropriate. They were suitable for teaching but this was the weekend after all. Already the Caribbean air was shifting my outlook on things, and that included the way in which I welcomed the potential for a breeze to penetrate my clothing. A loose, sleeveless dress was just what I needed.

Though her actions and language were foreign to me, Micheline made my stay at the teachers' house somehow less strange. With each day, I realized more how the accommodations might have made me uneasy and considered which of my colleagues back home would find them acceptable should they agree to teach a short course at UNOGA. Electricity was available only a few hours each evening, thanks to a generator. There was no internet access, but conversations with people who lived nearby were possible, at least until 8:30 or 9:00. In bed upstairs and armed with a flashlight, I read every word of the *New York Times* I had brought with me at least three times, even memorizing a recipe for compote I anticipated making once I returned to the October Midwest. I had intended to write while there, but preparing for and conducting classes drained me of my intellectual capacities. So, I read myself to sleep.

Netting draped around my bed, more for keeping away bees than mosquitoes, for a hive hung just outside one of my windows. The windows were tall and covered not with screens but with heavy wooden shutters that were difficult to latch. Neighboring houses were separated by vegetation, but I carefully closed the shutters each evening, trying not to give too much thought to what might take an opportunity to enter. Walking down the old wooden staircase in the middle of the night made me a bit nervous but that is where the lone bathroom was located. The toilet was not operational but the sink faucet was, though I was less interested in filling a bucket to flush manually than I was in running back upstairs to climb under the covers. I was staying in the house alone. Micheline would arrive very early each morning to begin preparing breakfast.

A large rodent seemed to scurry across the tin roof as I tried to fall asleep and convince myself they could not possibly find its way into my room. But I knew better. Years before, I had worked in the office of a domestic violence shelter on the south side of Chicago where the residents told us of their encounters with rats. Mine was a day job, so I had not seen them – only mice dropping on the keys of my typewriter when I came into work.

"Are you sure they're not mice?" I asked the women.

"They're not mice," they assured me. "They wake up our babies at night." It took some effort and a bit of adjustment in the budget, but we found a way to patch holes with wire mesh and plaster to the problem. We occupied a former convent of three stories donated to us by the Archdiocese. It was an incredible gesture for which the shelter director was eternally grateful, but some of the structure had devolved into a state of disrepair and demanded tremendous upkeep. Old buildings have their charm until modern residents are witness to their flaws.

The solution at the teachers' house was to add a cat, but the cat added was still a tiny kitten and undoubtedly incapable of confronting any rodents the size of what I heard on the roof. The wood flooring and trim was marked with holes through which something might squeeze, but I closed my eyes to make them disappear. Except for the scratching, the night was quiet. I wondered why I was not more afraid, alone on the second floor of this house situated in a tree-filled area home to voodoo practitioners. But I am never very afraid. Not really.

During the early evening after Micheline showed me my freshly-washed panties I took some time to take in the view from the balcony looking out toward the sea. The sun was just beginning to lower, changing the color of the sky to a warm yellow against the horizon. It truly was beautiful there. I held the railing and admired the many coats of paint beneath my hands, contemplating the history of the home – the ghosts. Not ghosts in a threatening sense, though Haiti had more than its share of past violence; just whatever lingered from earlier times spent there. I smiled and turned back to walk inside to take off my work clothes and lie down on the bed for a short time before dinner. Before I stepped in, something caught my eye in the sun's rays, which were streaming into the corner just a few feet from where I stood. It was a machete – a rusty machete standing against the outside wall. Anyone who knows Caribbean history realizes the prominent role machetes have played in all aspects of culture, but I wondered what it was doing on the second floor balcony. I considered it a good thing, for I dared not consider it anything else. I prayed it would act as a symbolic shield for me against any danger. In doing so, I noticed the nature of my prayers had changed. No longer did I find myself overcome or brought to tears; rather, I was in a state of calm, reflecting on the years that had brought me to this moment.

I lay on my bed as the aroma of dinner preparations floated up the staircase. The sound of music arose from a neighbor's CD player, growing louder until it filled the space between the houses and through the trees. It was Schubert's *Ave Maria*. There was a time when I fantasized about being married in a church and making the traditional walk to the statue of Mary, as brides do, while a full choir lifted their voices to *Ave Maria*. But those days were gone. Such a wedding was not in the stars. The piece still evoked feelings of love and I lay still, sensing its universality among the world's Catholic and non-Catholic people.

After dinner I sat on the porch and conversed with Micheline's daughter. She was an engaging teenager who wanted very much to practice her English with me. I happily obliged. She taught me Creole words for house and chair and tree, among other things, all of which I soon forgot. My language learning depends on sentences and practice and for some reason writing things down, and I'm afraid I did not make much progress. But it was delightful talking with her. I saw as much joy in her eyes seeing me try as I felt in watching my own students. Her English skills were notably advanced, and I asked her whether she would like some books to help her learn some more. She was thrilled.

The friends at work who had been kind enough to donate books for English language learners and their teachers expected me to pass them on to someone who would make good use of them. Though I had brought all I could possibly carry, distributing them to students would have required some difficult choices. If I were able to bring more, they might have been a nice addition to the small campus library. They seemed of no use to the lecture interpreters, as their English was already so good. But they were perfect for Micheline's daughter. She took the with much appreciation. Each day she came to me to show the exercises she had completed and report what she had learned. Micheline stood over her, clearly pleased with her progress.

In discussions at my home campus prior to this visit a thoughtful and caring faculty member criticized UNOGA's program for emphasizing English lessons. English, she warned, was a language of colonialism and historical domination. To be honest, I resented her tone. She was speaking to me as if I had no sense of historical power structures. Of course I understood the politics of language, I thought to myself as she glared at me. In Guatemala, for example, the recognition of indigenous languages during the 1990s peace process was fundamental to the acceptance of a vast proportion of the population. And that was just one case illustrating how significantly the tide was changing. But to deny accessibility to the increasingly global language of English would only hinder improvement in underdeveloped regions. Replacing Creole was not our aim.

At the same time, I was increasingly ashamed of my

inability to communicate in Creole. One of my very last memories of Haiti before the earthquake was sitting in the impressively modernized Port-au-Prince airport, listening to an American man boast of his contributions to the country. I am not inclined to eavesdrop, but it was impossible not to hear him. His voice was deep and carried through the entire waiting area. He represented an evangelical church in a very small town somewhere in the Dakotas and had made more than forty trips to Haiti primarily to build Christian churches, which he said were "sorely needed." His millionaire son donated the funds for a truck to haul building materials. He was particularly proud to be the father of a millionaire. A kind, middle-aged Haitian couple served as a captive audience and listened patiently to his stories.

"Do you speak Creole?" the woman softly interrupted.

"Nah," he replied. "Never took the time to try. But it didn't keep us from getting our work done." How crass, I thought, judging him as a typical ugly American imposing his language as well as his religion. And here I sat on my third trip to Haiti and looking at Micheline and not knowing what to say.

42
SAYING GOODBYE

Our last class together ended early. Perhaps I was a bit overwhelmed with the task of covering so much ground in so little time. On the other hand, I was satisfied that we had been able to accomplish a great deal. Their final essays came flooding in, one after the other, and I looked forward to grading them when I returned home. The task was a bit unnerving; the vast majority had written in French. I had encouraged them to do so because I did not want their thinking processes to be stifled by language limitations. It was better that I struggle in grading them than they struggle in writing them.

I thought they would look forward to ending our time together early; after all, American students would. But they did not. They wanted to stay, and they wanted me to stay. They asked that I spend some time helping them to practice their English and sat me on a chair on the raised area, elevated above their desks. It was a bit uncomfortable, as only about 40 or 50 students remained and I could have easily sat among them, but they said they preferred it that way. Even though they insisted that I converse with them, once we were situated they seemed quite shy. Strange, I thought, as they appeared so eager to keep me there to work on their skills. But as can be the case in any classroom, no one wanted to speak first.

Once the ice was broken however, they fired away, students joking about one another's inquisitiveness and courage to formulate questions in English. The less daring relied on the interpreter, who carefully gave me the questions. This interpreter was different from the others – a young man not much older than the students. In fact, I mistook him for a student that morning. I even mistook him for a Haitian. I should have known better, for a longer look revealed a swagger and a stance with an attitude so common in urban America. He was from Boston, he told me, born in Haiti but living the last dozen or so years in Boston. He had returned to Haiti just before the earthquake to live with family because things had not been working out for him. I tried to imagine what sorts of challenges he had faced – or what kind of trouble he had gotten into – to make Jeremie the better option for him. He worked hard to impress me in the post-class session and it became clear that he wanted to dictate who asked what and which questions I should answer. No matter, I thought, since the subjects were pretty mundane. I fielded inquiries about my town, my work, my activities, and my family. And then one wanted to know why I got divorced. The interpreter looked at me and told me not to answer.

"Why not?" I asked.

"It is none of their business," he replied. I was not sure why the question bothered him more than it bothered me, but I realized how difficult it would be to answer. I just smiled and said that I had three wonderful children from the marriage. My answer did not differ much from those I had given to acquaintances back home. Better to leave it at that, I thought.

The topic turned to politics, and they asked me to comment on the state of Haitian affairs. The election was approaching, just a little more than a month away. There was still a diverse array of candidates and I could not predict which way it might go, let alone which way it should go. Their experiences were better than mine, I reminded them, and the country's political history was more complex for me.

"I'm sorry. Your country's political situation is very interesting, I must say, but I don't know how to answer that." I did not feel equipped to comment. In retrospect, it probably seemed an appropriate response. But the truth was I did not know how to comment, and it is rare that I am left without words.

"Politicians don't do anything," one student commented. "They just make promises."

"Yes, they just want to win," added another.

Their cynicism was disheartening but understandable. The same sentiment exists among American college students and here, ten months following the earthquake, their government buildings remained in shambles and an estimated 1,000,000 Haitians were still living in tents. But my primary intention in coming to Haiti before the earthquake had been to explore how civic engagement might be inspired through education. Learning about democracy and the potential that existed within representative governments was indeed infused in their history and social studies curricula. And I wanted to do my part in helping to reinforce that at the college level.

While the Grand'Anse may seem absent from the radar of policy makers in Port-au-Prince, much of my intention in going there was to help in regional development outside the capital and empower young people to play leading roles in making things better. That is why I emphasized economic development, the struggles for independence, and the establishment of self-government in my lectures and assignments. The course of history has changed where individuals or groups of people have taken the future into their own hands, I showed them. As much as the powers that be might resist in order to maintain the status quo, situations can be changed. As a "democrat with a small d" I try to instill in my students the idea that change can come from them. I hoped this had not been lost on my UNOGA students.

"I can understand why you are frustrated, but if the politicians in Port-au-Prince aren't making things better, who can?" It did not take long for them to respond, but their answer was not at all what I expected.

"God!" a number of them shouted. I felt as if I were leading a revival meeting. Their belief in God was amazing. But their apparent dependence on God for solutions was, to be honest, discouraging. I sat in silence for a moment, but could not leave the conversation there.

"But these are worldly problems," I reminded them. To many of them the earthquake itself was viewed as an act of God, but I wanted them to see that the response to the devastation was in the hands of man. "How does God work in the world?" I asked, yielding to their approach, and again sat in silence.

"Through us?" one student asked.

In an instant, years of my own post-secondary education through which I learned of the world's religions and their attempts to explain man's relationship to a higher power came flooding back. So, too, did my years teaching the basics of the Renaissance, Reformation, and Counterreformation in world history classes, highlighting the conflicts between denominational positions on faith and good works. I knew that I was not here to teach religion any more than I had been hired to do so in the States. I can teach about religion, but this was crossing the line and it was almost time to go.

"Maybe," I replied. "I don't know." And I didn't know. There was no satisfactory answer. In a way, I knew I was really asking the question of myself and not of them.

"Is there anything you want to know about us?" a student asked.

"Hmm..." There were so many things I wanted to know, and I was grateful for the change in subject. "I would like to know more about voodoo." I was sincere. Some students laughed nervously, while others gasped and sunk back in their seats.

"No," said the interpreter, staring at me. "You shouldn't ask about that."

"What do you mean? I'm very curious."

"You shouldn't be curious about such things. It's dangerous."

"Voodoo is dangerous, or curiosity about it is?" Now I was laughing nervously. He was so serious. On one of our rides outside of town, Renate and I had seen a group of people dressed in white engaged in some sort of ritual. We knew of voodoo's prevalence, and accepted it as part of the culture. I just wanted to get a better sense of it all from a Haitian perspective. But the students seemed hesitant to talk about it.

"Everything about it," he replied. "Someone once put a curse on me and a demon came to visit." I looked at him, puzzled. I knew that he had lived much of his young life in Boston.

"Here?" I asked.

"I don't want to talk about it." He was tough and had seemed to find some pleasure in confronting me in a way possible only from a young American male. I stood up to look him in the eye, just in case he wanted to say more. "It had wings. It came through the window of my room."

"In Boston?" I wondered just how vibrant the Haitian immigrant community was there. His strong exterior softened and he looked shaken.

"It's ok," I reassured him. "We don't have to talk about it." Suddenly a female student ran into the classroom. I thought she had left for home.

"Teacher!" she called to me. I was getting used to being called that, but I turned with a jolt. The thought of a winged demon frightening this you man had set me on edge. "Oh, I am sorry to interrupt you."

"No, it's ok. What is it?"

"We have a surprise for you!" Others appeared behind her, holding wrapped packages.

"What?" They really did take me by surprise.

"We could not let you leave without goodbyes and some gifts." All of the students remaining burst into applause. I realized their request to practice English was a ploy to stall so they could finish preparing them.

"You don't have to give me gifts," I told them. They were so excited.

"Open them!" I was embarrassed. Teaching is what I do and it had been a long time since a group of students had seemed so grateful. "Open them!"

I carefully opened each one. There was a piece of local driftwood decorated with shells and some fossilized coral. I liked the idea of having pieces from the sea to take home with me. There was also a small, hand-embroidered cloth, decorated with palm trees and the word "Jeremie." It reminded me of the Caribbean souvenirs I had found among my father's things when I was a little girl. And last, there was a loaf of warm bread, fresh from the oven. I looked to the doorway and saw the women who prepared lunch for us each day standing there, smiling. It must have taken them all morning to bake it. As I opened its paper covering just a little to take a peek, the aroma of coconut and nutmeg filled my senses. It was glorious.

"Have a taste!" the students commanded.

"No, I couldn't eat it in front of you."

"We know what it tastes like. Try it while it is warm." I did. It tasted even more wonderful than it smelled, if that were possible.

Saying goodbye was very difficult, but it was time. I stepped down and they gathered around me.

"Promise you will come back," more than one pleaded.

"I would love to," I said, trying very hard not to make a promise I might not be able to keep. "If I can come back, it won't be for a while. I have students back home who are waiting for me."

As usual, Magalie and students piled into the back of the truck for our ride back. I sat quietly, trying to encapsulate every moment. I looked into my briefcase to make sure I had gathered all of my papers and books and caught a glimpse of small slips of paper with students' writing on them. They were course evaluations I had asked them to give me. It is common practice back home and I wanted them to become accustomed to the practice of giving feedback. I pulled out a few and read them.

"Dear Teacher, I love you and your class."

"Dear Teacher, God has blessed us with a very good teacher."

"Dear Teacher, Thank you very much. May God be with you on your journey."

"May God help you in your work always."

I did not know what to make of their comments but they made me feel wonderful. They were unlike anything I would hear from students back home. And again, I wasn't sure what to make of their acknowledgement of God at every turn. I did know, however, that I might need to rely on Him/Her to help me grade papers written in French.

43
RETURN

While at the Jeremie airport on my return flight
to the capital, I chatted with Magalie. She was gracious enough
to drive me to the airport and stay with me until the plane
boarded, even though it had been delayed an hour. I would
have been perfectly content to use the time people-watching.
It was something Renate and I had done there before, guessing
where the travelers had come from and what their business
in Haiti might be. We laughed as we recognized our own
stereotypes of American clergy and French doctors. On this
day the airport was rather quiet, but there was one charismatic
man about my age, dressed in cargo shorts and a wrinkled shirt.
He was surrounded by a group of people who were listening
intently to him tell a story. I was not near enough to hear what
he was saying, or whether he was speaking in English, but he
seemed to be relating how he got the huge gash on his leg.
He was very attractive and a few days past due in shaving. I
fantasized that he had been to Haiti on a medical mission and
had injured himself trying to help someone.

Magalie sat with me, wanting to be certain what time
the plane left so she could notify a man named Jean that I was
on my way. I was not sure who he was, but she had arranged
for him to meet me in Port-au-Prince. She had been so patient

all week with my poor language skills but we grew to like each other very much, and wanted to use our last time together having a conversation. We did so in Spanish, laughing much of the time. We still had a hard time communicating.

A couple of men sitting close to us were engaged in an intense conversation in Creole. Magalie could not help but listen in at the same time she was trying to converse with me. Soon she was adding her opinion. They were talking about politics and the future of the country. The tone was passionate but positive, though it was clear they were frustrated with the way things were being done – or not being done. Magalie became as animated as the others and her speech became faster and faster. It was mesmerizing to watch her. Most of the Haitian women I had come to know seemed to hold back in expressing their opinions, but not Magalie. Even she laughed when she saw me noticing how excited she had become. As the conversation came to an end, they sat back and shook their heads and Magalie offered a brief summary for me.

"Politicians just make promises," she said, and then repeated back to the men in Creole. They all nodded.

She spoke to Jean on her cell to make final arrangements for meeting me in Port-au-Prince. I asked her if he would be carrying a sign with my name on it. Making my way through the crowd of Haitians offering to carry my bags and give me rides was easier if I could see precisely who was there for me. She laughed and said she would describe me to him.

"A t-shirt of aqua blue," she said, after looking me up and down.

I was the last to board the plane and only one seat remained – next to the attractive man in the cargo shorts with a gash in his leg. I was certain it was fate. He was as dashing as Indiana Jones and must have been completing a good will visit of some kind. My mind wandered into a state of make-believe, but I knew this was a real opportunity to meet a real man and get my mind off the fantasy that had moved to California. As we situated ourselves I heard him speak English, with some sort of an East Coast accent. Sure, I would move to the East Coast for the man of my dreams, given the man of my dreams was a genius do-gooder risking injury to save the world. My youngest was nearly finished with high school, after all.

He pulled a camera with a very large lens from his bag and proceeded to take photographs through the window as the plane climbed higher. I looked around him to see Jeremie growing smaller and smaller. The vastness of its lush greenery and beautiful trees glistened in the clear air of early afternoon. It had, indeed, been a good trip. I looked more closely at the camera he held. It was impressive, and while a rich doctor might have been able to afford it, I got the impression he might be a journalist. Perhaps a journalist sent on a mission to capture the lives of the people we were leaving behind.

"If you don't mind, may I ask why you were in Jeremie?" While destiny had brought us together, it was up to me to act on it. He wasn't wearing a ring.

"I'm a birdwatcher," he replied, a little sheepishly.

"Really?" I wasn't sure how to respond. He suddenly looked more like Miss Jane Hathaway on the Beverly Hillbillies, decked out in her bird watching gear.

"It's sort of a hobby for me. I like to travel to different places to watch them migrate."

I love birds, but of all the things happening in Haiti I never would have imagined bird migration could draw someone there. He proceeded to tell me about the different varieties he had spotted. Perhaps I was destined not to spend the rest of my life with this man I was seated next to, but to stop and appreciate birds a little bit more.

When I arrived in Port-au-Prince, I understood why Magalie was amused by my concerns about Jean finding me. I had forgotten that flights from Jeremie arrived at the regional airport, not the international one, so among the sixteen or so people leaving the plane, it was pretty easy to pick out Kathy, the U.S. professor. He seemed to be performing this task as a favor on a day he had better things to do. I had changed my flight back from Sunday to Saturday in order to guarantee connecting back to Miami, but Saturday was a day a work in the capital, especially for a man in his position. He was a manager or a business owner of some kind and he asked if I would mind if we stopped by his work on our way to the hotel, as he had something to tend to. It was no problem for me. There was no place I needed to be.

Our drive through the city was frustrating for him. Traffic was horrendous. He wore dark, pressed pants and a short-sleeved dress shirt. It was warm and sweat shone on his forehead. He tried to be a gracious conversationalist and told me of his college experiences in Montreal. His command of English and worldly sensibilities set him apart and he told me how many educated professionals of his age had left the country at that time, never to return. But he said he recognized how Haiti was suffering severe brain drain and felt a duty to come home after college and apply the business skills he learned to help the economy. His was a food packaging business devoted primarily to freezing fish and fruit. We pulled up to the loading dock area and he jumped out.

"I will be just a minute," he promised. I took my calendar from my purse and looked at the days ahead. There was much to do before I returned to my classes on Monday. I looked up to see him talking with a group of impeccably uniformed workers who stood with respect in his presence. He listened and gave direction making it clear that he was a man who got things done. When he returned to the car he seemed relieved of only one of many duties.

"I want to thank you again for picking me up at the airport. I know this is a busy day for you," I told him.

"Oh, it is no problem, really," he assured me. "But I'm afraid the hotel room is not ready yet. Would you mind accompanying me on a few more errands?"

"No, not at all," I said. Hotel space had become gravely scarce since the earthquake. Many rooms had been destroyed, and those remaining were continuously filled with relief workers. Owners were able to charge incredibly excessive fees, and I knew I was fortunate that they were able to find me a room at all.

As we drove further, the streets became more congested. Jean took to listening to a talk radio station and stopped conversing. At first I thought he had work on his mind, but he was obviously captivated by the discussion. Immersed in French and Creole for more than a week, I was able to make out that the subject was politics. Even if I weren't able to, chances were good that the subject was politics. As is the case with Spanish and even reading in Italian and Portuguese, I can decode academic vocabulary comparatively easily. Ideas of democracy, representation, history, revolution, and so on are communicated with Latin-based words found across the Romance languages, as well as in English. Though I could not understand the details of what was being aired, I could tell this was an intellectual exchange of ideas that could affect the future of Jean's homeland.

He apologized for becoming engrossed in the program.

"It's no problem. It sounds interesting," I said.

"There are a lot of Haitians with a lot of ideas," he said. "I wish they could move faster in fixing these problems." He pointed to piles of rubble. "Look at all of these trucks! There were already traffic problems before they shipped in these trucks!" There were dump trucks filled with rubble all around us.

"It seems they've been able to clear the roads," I said.

"Yes, I am thankful for that. But they just keep moving the debris from one place to another. I don't know if they are making any progress." I knew how poor the conditions were before the earthquake and tried to imagine how bad things were in the days following.

"There is so much work to do."

"There are more people living here now than before the earthquake. They keep coming in and living on the streets with the hope of working for some cash being handed out by the relief workers. Look at these people! There is no place for them to live!" There were hundreds of people just within our view, who had set up blankets and mini-enterprises. "We would all be better off if there were something for them to do outside of the capital."

"That is what we are hoping in helping to develop the university in Dekade," I noted. "I know it's a long way off, but there is so much potential there."

"Yes, the potential for fruit production is amazing. Did you see the women carrying fruit to market in baskets each morning?"

"Yes, it was impressive."

"But there is so much waste. They can't possibly sell it all and it goes bad in a couple days."

"But look at all the people in Port-au-Prince. They need fruit," I said as if suddenly a business expert.

"Yes, the banana boats come in from Jeremie, but even then much of it spoils. I have talked with some people about building a packaging facility there, so the fish and fruit can be frozen on site."

"That would be wonderful!" I said, imagining the possibilities.

"But it can't be done without getting permission from the government." He shook his head. "And how fast do you think that would happen?"

The gridlock lightened up for just a moment, and we began to move. His eyes stared ahead. I saw in him a man of talent and accomplishment who felt paralyzed.

"Is the traffic always this bad?" I asked.

"Yes," he replied. "But at least the roads are clear. The earthquake left them piled high with bricks and concrete. I climbed and walked for hours, until the sun went down, looking for my family."

"They were ok?"

"Yes," he said softly. Finding them safe must have been a relief, but the pain of that day stayed with him.

We continued to the hotel in silence, passing collapsed buildings, thousands of tents, and many individuals trying to piece together their lives the best they could.

44
HISTORICAL CONTEXT

I continued my research about Haiti after returning home, but was not sure where to focus. Though the country's long and intricate history made the options endless, so much had changed as a result of the earthquake.

From time to time I ask my students to analyze a current event in a 3-4 page paper. I expect them to pay attention to what has been going on in the world during the semester, choose a particular issue, pull together four or five news articles from different sources, and write an analytical essay examining various perspectives, placing it into some sort of historical context. By the end of a history course it is my hope that they can understand a bit better how history has shaped the contemporary world. On a more philosophical level, I hope they can see how past, present and future are linked in one continuous thread. And I hope they can look at events appearing in the news today and more effectively determine which of them will one day be understood as historically significant.

The number of "news" sources to which they have access is astronomically greater than that of generations past, though the vast majority of what they are exposed to is genuinely irrelevant. This goes beyond celebrity news and reaches into what they are being told is science, serious political discourse, and so on. As is the case with many students in the U.S. ours are not required to take a course in information or media literacy which might better cultivate the skills needed to sift through what is being thrust upon them and decide what is true and not and what might have long term and far reaching effects. So I give them some places to start and hope they can find their way through a maze of world news sources and discover something they can deem historically relevant.

What is often the case with world news – and this was even more true before the advent of the internet – is that when we do get a story it is often due to some immediate calamity, usually a natural disaster. While I urge students to seek information regarding ongoing issues – for example human trafficking, child labor, or international trade agreements – I can bet that if there is a natural disaster during the semester up to a third of the students in the class will insist on writing about it. To prevent any dismissal of natural disasters in a way that might seem heartless, I merely suggest that if they do choose a devastating earthquake, hurricane, etc. as the subject of their paper, they need to be able to explain the potential historical significance of the event. Students are generally not equipped to do this, but I encourage them to take a leap. Natural disasters are not yet covered in much depth in history textbooks. There are ways, however, to consider their historical impact where social, economic, and political consequences are clear.

I kept this in mind when weighing possible research topics for myself, but it was difficult and my work came in fits and starts. As a historian who tried to resist presentism, I wanted to ignore the earthquake. My initial investigation had been in curriculum and education and part of me wanted to continue with that. Professionally, I could justify it based on my work with the Commission for Higher Education and in curriculum development endeavors on campus. But to take on a project so directly related to my interviews and observations of January 2010 was too painful.

In my discipline I felt an obligation to think historically, and various aspects of Haiti's 19th and early 20th century educational system interested me. I was fascinated by philosophies of learning surrounding the struggle for independence and attempts at transforming schools to meet the needs of the new republic. I also considered exploring what happened to schools during and after U.S. occupation. When I sat down with the sources, an abundance of information came to me effortlessly. But there were still moments in which I felt overwhelmed, almost strangled when it came to putting my ideas on paper. This had never happened to me before. The weight of the country and its problems were affecting me personally, and I felt powerless to contribute anything of value through my work.

At the same time, I found myself writing freely on the side in what one might call journaling. It seemed an extension of what I had begun alone in my room in Haiti in the days before the earthquake. At first I resisted, finding no worth in it aside from personal catharsis. But then I let it happen. I thought at the very least it would help get it out of my system so I could get down to business. Friends and family continued to ask me questions about my experiences, but casual conversation seemed insufficient for providing answers. When I looked into their eyes and around at our setting – the dinner table, my office hallway, or the grocery store – it was difficult to explain. I found myself responding to them on paper. And eventually I was able to go back to the academic sources.

The history of agricultural education kept my attention

for some time. It provided a unique viewpoint as Haiti always had been primarily an agricultural society. Examining the intentions of education there, with land development and food production serving as a backdrop, helped to make sense of how schools developed in the way that they did. There were sufficient materials on either the history of education or the history of agriculture, including both primary and secondary sources. But no one had yet interwoven the two stories. That is the work of the historian, and that is why history is always new. The more I let the idea percolate, the more excited I became.

When friends and colleagues asked what I was working on, I enthusiastically told them the history of agricultural education in Haiti. They generally looked back at me with less enthusiasm. This is not uncommon for the historian, as we are often immersed in projects others find unimportant or uninteresting. Our own enthusiasm and interest are what matters most and are usually enough to keep us going and see books and articles through to completion. But in this case people seemed to expect something different from me.

"I thought you would be writing about the earthquake," one friend commented.

"No, it's too recent," I replied. "I'm a historian. We need to wait at least twenty or thirty years to have any insight. We need to be removed from the event." Then I realized that perhaps I was trying to avoid something by losing myself in a project that had nothing to do with what I had experienced. What I should have been doing was facing it.

45
RESEARCH

When I took an honest look at my past strengths in research I knew they lay in various aspects of population policy. Much of it related to birth control history and I looked into the Haitian story just enough to see whether something there spurred some interest. This lead could take me in a direction that paralleled my early work on religion and birth control. But it did not address the earthquake directly in any way, and that is the path I knew I needed to take.

Immediately following the earthquake, one of former President Bush's advisors was asked how it could be possible that so many had died. He replied that too many people lived in Port-au-Prince to a large degree due to women's unwillingness to use birth control. This came through an interview within hours of the event, as I remember watching it at my parents' house just after I had left the airport. For him to make such a sweeping judgment, and so smugly and quickly, made my skin crawl. But when it came time to engage in substantive research, I did not want to give that position any kind of credence, even by attempting to disprove it.

Other research I had done focused on migration, but the most accessible information related to Haiti appeared to center on Haitians leaving the country. That was not the story

I wanted to tell, at least for now. I wanted to write something about the Haitians who had stayed in Haiti. When I looked a little closer, I came across materials discussing migration from the countryside to Port-au-Prince. Some of it had come from my initial look at agricultural education that had drawn students to the capital. But that was just part of it. I put it out of my mind for a while and took care of my daily responsibilities.

Numbly is how I approached the work, and numbly is how I was expected to remain in the work. Perhaps that is what took me so long to complete something from it. Because I could not. Digging into the research dredged up something, and I was going places for which I was not yet ready. It seemed the very idea of putting research to the test in an area so tangible, so close, had scared me.

I had become comfortable with the benefit historians have in the detachment that stems from observing and analyzing people, places, and things that existed long ago and far away. As valuable as the investigations might be, on a personal level there is a safety space. It is work very suitable for someone too sensitive for the here and now and for interactions with people alive. It allows for explanations of why things are the way things are and for an intimacy solely with humans who have left the planet. For those who can do both – live life among dust-laden documents and then chit chat with friends over tea or wine – it can be the perfect life. But there are times when things get intertwined, when one life is more difficult to leave behind at the end of the day. In the middle of research, one's mind can stay connected to the subject during all waking hours, giving the appearance of absent-mindedness or aloofness. While some academics seem to prefer this state because it relieves them of mundane tasks or normal relationships, for most it is not a choice. The call to history cannot be helped. And the detachment that research brings is just part of the work. However, detachment should not be mistaken for numbness. Nor vice versa.

Then one day while sitting in my living room, just being still and letting everything in my life take care of itself for the time being, it came to me: urban vulnerability. It was not the first time I had thought of it. My best research had been on urban vulnerability in the early Cold War and policy makers' successful attempts to inspire suburbanization to protect the U.S. population in case of atomic attack. This was before I had shifted my teaching to Latin America but I always knew there would be an opportunity to someday explore aspects of vulnerability there. Though my argument and evidence were solid, I had no success in publishing it until just after the attacks on New York and the Pentagon on September 11, 2001. Within weeks, the editors at the British journal *Cold War History*, where I had recently submitted the article, contacted me. Urban vulnerability was of dire concern.

Within only a few days of the Haiti earthquake, a professor of public policy from Purdue in West Lafayette contacted me and I told him I had written on urban vulnerability in the past and wanted to address the topic with Port-au-Prince in mind.

"I look forward to reading our work," he wrote. "Please let me know when it's finished."

Finished? At that point I could barely make it through the day. It was reported that within the past 18 months or so a Purdue geologist had predicted the possibility of an earthquake devastating to Port-au-Prince.He and his team had presented their work at a conference, but as is the case with scientists, the fruits of their labors do not always gets the public's attention. Even if the vulnerability of Port-au-Prince was unrecognized by almost everyone in the world it was still vulnerable, and I wanted to know how it came to be that way.

Once I allowed the story to be told, materials fell into my hands. My library of choice is the University of Chicago's Regenstein and during each visit I stacked what I could handle, determined to digest the maximum possible in one sitting. I wondered whether I might find more materials elsewhere, traveling to a university with a stronger geography department for example, but as long as I was finding what I needed, I just kept going. My skills in reading French were repeatedly challenged and I kept a dictionary beside me to use as needed. Many of the most useful resources were shelved on Level B, a sub-basement of the library, where I never believed I would feel so comfortable. I thrive on sunshine and feel my body and mind change without it. But here, underground, I grabbed all of the mental energy I could possibly muster.

Historical investigation is not unlike detective work and I remind my students of that as they flock to majors in criminal justice and forensics, based on what television portrays as captivating work. Digging up the truth on events of the past might not get the same level of attention, but what is the difference between the truth of yesterday, or ten years ago, or one hundred years ago, or one thousand years ago? Maybe I should refer to their history assignments as "cold cases."

But the devastation of Port-au-Prince was not a cold case, was it? It was perhaps the most open of cases I had tackled and that is what made the work so difficult. It was open, as in an open wound. I had distanced myself from it the best that I could, either consciously or subconsciously. To revisit the history was to unearth a city built without a strong foundation and then buried in the rubble. It would unearth human bodies, human grief, and the spirits that accompanied them. It was not my intention to uncover some conspiracy that purposely led so many to their deaths. I simply wanted to piece together the development of what might be termed urban vulnerability.

The fragile nature of urban existence in other parts of the world differed in historical development from that of the United States, where issues of vulnerability often centered on threats of enemy attacks. But in all cases, survival and functionality were at stake and where poverty was rampant the social and economic effects of destruction might be even worse. That was the case with Port-au-Prince. Much of the population was densely concentrated there, as were government administrative services, and economic infrastructure and decision-making. The ineffectiveness of agencies and the government made recovery more difficult, but it was that same ineffectiveness that allowed for unchecked growth and unregulated construction of homes and other buildings for the last half century.

There was not a clear path in putting together the story. It had not been told before, and this was one of those instances where the lack of documentation served as an important aspect of the story. The fact that there was so little attention paid to the possible consequences and documented attempts to plan for a more stable future. But very few knew of the potential for an earthquake there. And I needed to make that clear. After being holed up for hours in a corner of the library seemingly unnoticed to others, I emerged to log onto a computer among a sea of computers stationed in the wide open spaces of the first floor. Students were conducting research of their own, writing essays, and engaging in various types of social networking. They looked, perhaps, a little worn around the edges, but overall student-like. I on the other hand appeared a virtual bag lady, the multiple days' darkness paling my complexion and my most valuable belongings, plus lunch, in any number of briefcases and tote bags.

Immersion in research customarily results in fewer showers and more wrinkled clothing. Though I had not slept in my clothes, it became convenient to put on whatever I had thrown onto the chair in my bedroom the night before, and this was probably day number three. I sometimes imagine dressing all in white to write – clean shirt and pants – like Diane Keaton did in that film where she wrote plays and had sex with Jack Nicholson. I envied her dedicated walk to her beautiful and pristine work space each morning, looking out through a large picture window over the sunlit sea. Somehow I always found myself in much less glamorous writing situation.

One day a workman on a remodeling project at the Regenstein stopped me before I could place my hand on a freshly painted railing.

"Sir," he said. I only vaguely heard him, not knowing he was talking to me. "Be careful where you touch."

"Sir?" I thought, looking down at my baggy jeans, gray t-shirt graced with an Einstein quote, and hoodie. I had my hair up in my favorite baseball cap, which was the color of Georgia clay. From that point on I vowed never again to look completely like a man while working. Still, there was something reassuring about being non-descript, even invisible, while entering the realm of lives past.

This day, as I sat down at the computer in clear view, I was once again aware that no one around had any idea what was swimming around in my head. I wanted to find a report, conference paper, anything, that referenced the work of Purdue University scientists who knew of the seismic potential in Haiti.

Enter: google.com.

Enter: Purdue, Haiti, earthquake.

Search.

Find: Names.

Find: Academic search databases.

Enter: Names.

Enter: Purdue.

Enter: Haiti, earthquake.

Search.

There it was. I read through the abstract and into the article. My hands froze on the keys and then dropped to my lap. Tears fell down my cheeks and dripped from my chin. It was real and I was no longer numb.

46
REMINDERS

Life goes on and as months passed there were more and more days when I never even thought about Haiti. When it did cross my mind I was bothered by the fact that people continued to struggle in their rebuilding efforts while I had returned to my First World comforts. But unless I was going to devote my life to the country, it felt better this way. I continued to do what I could, spreading the word about the ongoing efforts of Haitian Connection and seeking grants to support the Université de la Nouvelle Grand'Anse. I was embarrassed to admit that I felt more at peace not thinking about it too much. Still, when I least expected it, there were reminders.

Occasionally there would appear news stories about Haiti and they often sought to illustrate how little progress had been made since the earthquake. That was disheartening – both that little progress was being made and that the news media deemed it necessary to continually point it out. Sean Penn was interviewed from time to time and it was impossible not to stop and admire the amazing work he was doing there. The context in which some reminders appeared, however, made the whole thing seem surreal.

I was finding trips to the gym more and more satisfying. My campus had a facility that suited me just fine, but it was good to work out away from campus at a place considerably more posh. Large windows let in morning sunlight that shone over the pool and swimming laps while bathed in it was a joy. So, too, were lying in the steam room or dry sauna. I went there to cleanse and distress. It was a form of meditation for me and it was the best way I knew to feel better about all things. I also liked what it did for my body.

When the weather was good, I would run on the outdoor track and follow up with a series of free weight exercises, my ipod carrying me away with Aretha Franklin or Dave Matthews. I added reps based on whether I had one glass of wine or two the night before and if I were planning to dine out later in the day. When the weather was not good, I would hit an elliptical machine, grabbing a fashion magazine for inspiration. It did not matter to me whether it was a year old; I was usually behind the curve when it came to style anyway.

One particularly dreary spring morning I reached for a *Smithsonian* instead. While stepping more quickly and watching my heart rate rise, an article caught my eye. It described the undying passion of Haitian artists and their attempts to cope post-earthquake by continuing to paint and sculpt. I felt my heart sink and I slowed my pace. I read only a few words from a few paragraphs, looked at a couple of photographs and stepped down to exchange the magazine for something else. Haiti would always be a part of me, but in order to carry on with my workout I needed to put it out of my mind. Concepts of physical labor and calorie consumption there were conflicting with what I needed to accomplish. A 60-minute workout, guilt free.

That summer, I found myself sitting with my sons at my mother's dining room table, watching the small television perched on the stand in the corner. I liked that my mom was an avid game show watcher in the late afternoon and only of shows where she had to use her brain. It was rare that any two of my children were in the same place at the same time anymore, so this was a treat. As their birthdays fell that week, just four days apart, she lured them over with a special meal of homemade macaroni and cheese, steaks on the grill, and her signature salad graced with her garden's first tomatoes of the year. It was a challenge physically and emotionally to ten to the garden during this first summer that my dad was gone so they were extra special.

We never eat with the television on but had arrived early with plenty of time to visit.

"Cash Cab Chicago!" Sam shouted. I was as excited as the boys were to see that it was on. I had never seen the Chicago version. A few days before, my aunt had called me out of the blue to ask if I was on Cash Cab. She had seen someone who looked exactly like me, from the side, on the street during a shout-out.

"No," I told her. "It wasn't me." But I secretly wished it had been. We chit-chatted for a while, making plans to attend my cousin's christening party for his new daughter, then said good-bye. I hoped the person who looked just like me had answered the question right.

I had stumbled upon Cash Cab a few times before, not knowing at what time or on what channel it aired. I am fascinated by it; not so much by the questions, though quiz games always suck me in. Rather, the whole idea of random people on their way to other things taking time from their lives to entertain us with their thinking skills and exposing us to their memory banks was captivating, though I suppose the possibility of winning money is what gets them to stop what they're doing. In any case, I liked seeing maps of New York and trying to match them with memories of my visits there, all the while fantasizing that I was the one riding in the cab. Not answering questions, but riding to the theater or to dinner and then to the theater.

Cash Cab Chicago promised an excitement of its own, as the streets were so familiar.

"Do you recognize any of those places?" my mom asked from behind the counter. She insisted that she didn't need any help getting dinner on the table.

"Not sure," Danny replied.

"I'm trying to hear," whispered Sam in my ear, hoping I could keep everyone's attention on the game.

"Haiti," I said. I don't remember what the question was, but the answer was Haiti.

The contestant got it right. I had a feeling he would. He seemed pretty geeky. Just the right kind of genuinely geeky to know all the answers to random questions.

"He looks like a University of Chicago student," said Danny.

"Yep." I wish I could remember the question. I had a hard time reconciling the juxtaposition between Cash Cab and Haiti, and that is all that stuck with me.

Being together with my mom and kids was good. I missed my dad, but he seemed to live on in the tomatoes from the garden. They were sweet and full of sunshine.

47
DR. N

The physician I see when need be is Nigerian and treats holistically. I first visited him years after having babies and being seen almost solely by OB-GYNs. I had not had a regular doctor since before I was married and if any issue unrelated to pregnancy or childbirth arose had been able to get prescriptions from my father-in-law, who was a thoracic surgeon. He was definitely old school, and I mean that in the kindest of ways. He genuinely missed the days of house calls and being paid in fresh sausages and such. That might have been rare for a thoracic surgeon, but it was something he learned from his father, a general practitioner who was old, old school, from what I understand. I never had the pleasure of meeting him. My father-in-law had done the occasional stitching on kitchen tables (he had a reputation of being better skilled at sewing his lawn mower grass catcher than doing conventional household repairs) and even removed a small growth from their pet standard poodle. In regular practice his approach was generally one of cutting people open to see what was wrong. I often wondered what he would have thought of my new doctor.

After the nastiness of office politics had taken a toll on my physical wellbeing, I went to see Dr. N. A friend of mine who had embraced natural health and alternative medicine once mentioned him and I knew when it came time to see someone I would seek him out. In that first appointment, he promptly put me on a fast. "Thou shalt detox" was his first commandment. He then sent me for blood work to have my levels of all sorts of things checked and within weeks balanced them all, adding high doses of vitamin D. I felt great. He frequently asked about my work and recommended I more often take a path of least resistance at the office and let myself shine in my giftedness. That was easier said than done, but I applied what advice I could. He also asked about my love life.

"It's ok," I would tell him, knowing that he knew better.

"You need to have sex more often," he would tell me, and at periodic visits asked how I was doing in that area.

"Fine," I would say.

"You will make someone a good wife someday," he told me. If I had heard that at any other time in my life I would have met it with resentment, but at this point it seemed a good time. Dr. N. just seemed to know when it was beneficial to hear certain things. At this age, independent and secure, I knew I would choose the right husband if it came to that.

"What are you working on this summer?" he asked in early 2011, knowing the spring semester was coming to an end.

"I'm writing a book about Haiti."

"Ahh..." He was sincerely interested and seemed to be interpreting the peace that showed in my face. We had talked about my writing projects before, but this one was different. "I love the Haitian people."

"Me, too," I responded. I was not sure "love" was the right word for my feelings toward the entire people of any country and wondered in what ways he might love them, and to what degree.

"You know, many of them came from my people in Africa, the Igbo." I did not know that, but looked deep into his dark eyes, as if through them, and into the matter of his mind. I suddenly pictured the matter liquefying into blood, flowing through his veins, down his arms, out his fingertips, and meeting with the endless, rough waters of the Atlantic. Fixed on his eyes, my peripheral vision held the color of his skin in soft focus. "And they were taken to the Caribbean."

I loved my visits to his office and wondered whether it was because he had a way of hypnotizing me. I wanted him to transfer all that he knew from generations of presence on the planet, or from some sort of universal energy of knowledge, from his mind into mine. I wanted to understand all that he understood, beyond my book learning, lecture note taking, and physical visits to the country. I wanted to know what he knew.

"What is the title of your book?" he asked. Titles should not matter at this point, I thought, and they can certainly change at any time before publication. I considered it a strange question.

"*Brush with Haiti*," I said. For some reason I did already know what the title would be, and it was not simply a working title. It was helping to frame the book, not so much providing a structure as it was painting a backdrop that gave me the serenity to keep writing.

"*Brush with Haiti*," he repeated.

"Because I have studied it and taught about it and have been there, but I don't feel that I really know it, or anything about it, or ever will. Certainly not well enough to write a book about it, but I can't seem to stop writing."

He knew I had been there. I made a visit to his office just before my trip preceding the earthquake. I was due for a checkup and asked about malaria preventative and possible immunizations. On my trip with the bishop we had been advised to prepare for malaria and have the series of Hepatitis shots, as well as tetanus, and I complied.

"You're healthy, aren't you?" he asked as if to remind me. "You're feeling well?"

"Yes." He recommended a nutrition-dense pro-biotic powder to mix with my drinking water every other morning.

"That should keep your gut working properly. And just eat natural foods while you're there. That shouldn't be too difficult. You will be fine."

When his nurse came into the examination room and found out I was traveling to Haiti, she asked for a favor.

"Would you bring me back a shot glass? Every time I know someone traveling to another country, I ask them to bring me a shot glass. I have them from all over the world now, but none from Haiti." I did not doubt that. Visits to Haiti are rarely of the shot glass kind and this one would be no different.

"Sure," I said. "I'll see what I can do."

I figured I would try once I got back to the airport gift shop, but did not give it much more thought. However, in the artisans' cooperative where Renate took me on our last day before the earthquake, there they were – hand painted and beautiful. I looked carefully at the variations in style and the colors chosen, trying to decide between the simple brush-stroked houses and palm trees or flowers and birds. I found myself spending far too much time contemplating the perfect one, but finally made a selection along with my bracelet and other things.

She was very pleased and surprised that I had even remembered. As I handed it to her she looked as if she had seen a ghost, and mumbled something about the earthquake.

Yes, it was true. I just missed it, but had not forgotten her request. I wondered whether she would actually use it and thought maybe it was for wheatgrass or something, since she worked for Dr. N. and all. Now, more than a year later, that exchange seemed so far in the distant past.

"I'm writing a book, too," Dr. N. told me.

"About what?" I asked.

"Slavery."

I looked again at his skin and eyes. He had migrated from Africa a century after slavery had ended and under different circumstances. I was interested in his take on it. His understanding of the world in general and happenings in it transcended the material and always reach toward the good. His story was sure to acknowledge the gruesome history and horrid individual accounts yet conclude something unique and not yet stated. I looked forward to it, whatever it might be.

"I don't understand what has happened to the Haitian people. They have the same blood and yet they have not been able to succeed. We have always been the entrepreneurs."

"Slavery happened," I reminded him, as if that needed to be said. "Though Haitians were the first in the Americas to abolish it."

"It's true," he said, nodding. "You know," he continued, "it is as if they are still enslaved mentally. Imagine this: Someone places a very heavy chain on one leg of a baby elephant so all it can do is walk in one small circle. Then the elephant grows into a strong adult, the chain is cut and a much smaller one, attached to nothing, is put in its place. The elephant might continue to walk in one small circle, believing it is limited and not knowing its own power. I am afraid that is what has happened to the Haitian people." His ease with the animal story fascinated me. "In my homeland, we lived with animals. We were not treated as animals."

I recalled the entrepreneurial spirit and accomplishments of the Haitians I had met. On a larger scale, however, their potential for economic development appeared still shackled.

"So how is your sex life?" he asked. "Are you still California dreaming?" I had confessed some time before that I never quite got over my former love who had moved to California. "California is beautiful. My brother lives in a huge house on a very large piece of land high on a mountain. You can see forever."

He put one hand on my shoulder and the other just below my collar bone. Then he pounded three of his fingers hard into my chest, just left of center.

"How does that feel?"

"Ok," I replied, knowing that he knew exactly what he was doing to me. My heart began fluttering and the chest area surrounding it became warm.

"You know, there is just one source of love energy that manifests itself in many ways and in many people. If you open your eyes you will find someone else."

Really, I thought.

"Allow yourself to feel it again." I wondered whether a new love would walk into my life or whether my love for Haiti would be reignited in some way.

Dr. N.'s office is usually filled with patients waiting for what has sometimes seemed an eternity, and this is why. He engages with each one of them far more than any doctor I have known. On this day, I was his last patient, so he and I let the conversation meander, but I knew his devoted office staff was waiting to get out of there.

On my way home, I remembered reading something

about the practice of tapping and realized he was treating my
heart. He must have known that if he had asked my permission,
I might not have given it.

48
Home

The women I eventually came to know who worked through their churches on various activities were truly impressive and those of Westminster Presbyterian were no exception. They invited me to speak to their Missions Committee about the projects developed by Haitian Connection. The group included a friend and neighbor, her sister, my former student Heleine who was born in Haiti, and an incredibly involved community leader and wife of a prominent attorney, among others. Westminster was well-known for its active engagement, and it was no surprise that the parking lot was nearly full on this Wednesday evening. In addition to a variety of well-attended committee meetings, the preschool was hosting an open house. I remembered how unwelcome I had felt at the St. Thomas More Peace and Social Justice meeting I first attended and suddenly realized that it was not due to the women there who were, in fact, exceptionally dedicated. It was me. That was at a time in my life when I had let any sense of self-worth be undermined. Things were different now.

They opened the meeting with a prayer and then corrected and approved the minutes of the last meeting. For some reason I had been quite nervous about the talk, perhaps because my friends were there. I had planned and replanned a PowerPoint presentation in my head, with photos, maps, and some explanation of the work of Haitian Connection, then decided against it altogether. It was a relief to find there was no projector available anyway. There I sat with the nicest group of women you would ever want to meet, around a conference table at what I had known as the church down the street when I was growing up. It was where I attended Girl Scout meetings and attained my Red Cross First Aid certification. Though remodeled, I could remember where it was that I learned how to start a fire, sail against the wind, find the North Star, apply a tourniquet, and even suck the venom from a snake bite.

I spoke for what I thought was only about ten minutes, maybe fifteen, because they had other matters to take care of at the meeting. It is likely that I went over, as professors are accustomed to speaking an hour and twenty minutes at a pop, twice a week, times two to four classes, on any number of topics. Perhaps I did not go into great detail in my effort to keep within the time limit. Whatever I said was a blur, and then I sat. It was silent. There was a seeming gulf between us. Had I made a mistake of some kind? Was it because I had been there and they hadn't and I failed to make something clear? Was my Catholicism showing through? Was it something else I said? Then the questions began. We ended up conversing for perhaps 40 minutes or more. They wanted to know so much and in the end expressed a desire to donate enough money to have a house built.

The houses being designed through Haitian Connection were simple, useful, and once occupied, beautiful. Of painted concrete block, they provided a living area, kitchen, and bedroom for a woman and her family. Women in Haiti are often the primary breadwinners, and families, the community, and the general economy depend upon them. For a woman to have a secure home for herself and her children can help to lay a more stable foundation for the future. I think the Westminster women recognized this and saw funding the project as one considered "woman to woman."

Some months went by and when arrangements were finally made to hold their final fundraising brunch, I was feeling quite detached from the project, though I did not know why. To be part of such an act of kindness, even in a tangential way, should have brought some dimension of enjoyment. In fact, I was unequivocally unhappy. Again, it was due not to the project but to my own circumstances. As absurd as it is, we too often see matters through a prism of our own concerns.

Sam was preparing to leave for college downstate and I was in the final stages of selling my own home. It was a 3-bedroom mid-century modern split level. I had bought it a couple years after my divorce, in order to move on with my life. It broke my heart knowing that I had broken my children's hearts by selling their childhood home. But this new one was brick and plaster, built solidly into the earth and surrounded by mature trees. I wanted it to give me stability and security and proof that I could manage on my own when others believed I could not. I wanted to show my children that I could provide; that they could depend on me. It took a tremendous amount of work, as it was in need of serious updating, which in turn took a tremendous amount of time and money. I underestimated how difficult it would be to keep my head above water, especially with unforeseen strains in the housing market, and in the end I had very little equity left. But I did it. The first years we were there were hard and I tried not to let my kids see me cry, so I would hold back the tears until my head hit the pillow.

And now I was letting that part of my life go. My mother kept referring to me as an empty-nester. When I had first heard that term years before, I imagined being an empty nester together with someone someday. But that was not to be. It was a great house, but I could not imagine living in it by myself. The time to go had come.

On the bright side, this would be the time when I might move to an apartment in downtown Chicago and make the reverse commute to campus. Apartment hunting had become new to me again when I interviewed for a position as Executive History Producer at C-SPAN two years before. Hours of sifting through apartment listings online and dreaming of living in D.C. turned into days and then into weeks. The time between interviews was torture, and long before I was informed that I did not get the job, I realized that maybe what I truly wanted to do was sell the house and bring the suburban chapter of my life to an end. The man for whom I was still holding a torch had lived in a downtown high-rise when I met him. Though the relationship had long since ended, I yearned for the feeling of his surroundings, his view, and believed that just about 650 square feet overlooking Lake Michigan was just what I was missing. But accepting an offer on the house and seeing a tentative closing date in print made it all too apparent that no dwelling could act as a substitute for him.

Memories of an evening on the porch of the teachers' house in Jeremie flooded my mind. I had finished for the day. The air was warm and clear and preparations were underway to run the generator for the evening. But there was no need yet for electric light. The sun had not quite set and it was good to be off my feet and rocking in the chair for just a bit.

Micheline's daughter stepped onto the porch, just as my eyes began to close.

"There is someone here to see you," she said.

"Who is it?" Before she could answer, Francois of the Agricultural Ministry walked through the door from the kitchen. I had enjoyed chatting with him a few days before.

"Hello," he said in a soft voice. "Is it okay to visit you now?"

"Sure," I said, rising clumsily from my chair.

"Please, do not get up."

I had become accustomed to the practice of people dropping in for a conversation, imagining how life was before television and telephones. My kids enjoyed friends dropping by but had usually made arrangements through their smart phones, leaping from the table after reading a text alerting that a friend had arrived and was waiting in the driveway. To simply rest, thinking with one's eyes closed and having someone stop in for conversation, was nice.

"So, how is your class going?" he asked.

"Well, I think. The students are wonderful. Just wonderful." From there, we discussed all sorts of things, from our families to global politics.

"So, you are divorced?" I was hoping he had not picked up on that part. It was not worth mentioning.

"Yes."

"For how long?" he asked.

"Nine years."

"And you never married again?"

"No." I'd been amply warned about Caribbean men and possible expectations of U.S. women, and tried to remember what I had been told about Haitians, particularly their attitudes toward marital relationships. But he seemed genuinely curious and he spoke very fondly of his wife.

"I do not think people should be alone." His comment

struck a nerve. "Do you?"

"I don't know," I replied. But I did know. For some time, being alone had been the right thing for me. It was a necessary part of the process of detachment, and, in my case, of proving that I could make it on my own. But I was detached now, and no longer had anything to prove.

"No. People should not be alone." He was certain. In another time in my life I would have objected to his assertion and his certainty, arguing that someone might very well choose to be independent. Yes, arguing. But I did not argue so much anymore. There was a time when I might have believed that his position was one of an old-fashioned male and that he should try harder to understand the modern age, regardless of whether this was a cultural difference and that Haitians were more comfortable with traditional gender roles.

But his words did not seem to originate from any sort of male stance. Rather, they were simply human. In a heartbeat, I recognized something soulful. He was not suggesting that a woman could not survive on her own. He needed only to look around any Haitian neighborhood to see how women had taken responsibility. Rather, he seemed to say that women needed men just as much as men needed women. Or that the ideal relationship was one in which two people complemented one another, and were there for one another, and brought out the best in one another. But all he said was, "I do not think people should be alone." What I heard was much more, and undoubtedly stemmed from my own need to hear.

"I'm waiting for the right person."

"I understand. But do not wait too long."

No one could substitute for the right person, and no apartment in the city could substitute for the person who had introduced these emotions to me.

"I could live in a box on State Street with you," I once told him. And it was true. The trappings of the material world seemed meaningless in comparison to the raw connection I felt with him. And he was more intellectually stimulating and entertaining than anyone I had ever met. And he filled my soul. Living with a city view that we once shared could not replace him. It could not fill the void. I realized it would only make me feel worse. My house was large and empty but a city apartment would be small and empty.

It was good to see the members of the Westminster Mission Committee at the brunch. The turnout was wonderful and they asked me to get up and say a few words. I did. Then I happily sat with them and we talked about kids growing up and the process of returning to who we were before they entered our lives. We would be forever changed by the experience of motherhood, but there was pleasure in rediscovering ourselves once we were less busy and had time to breathe. My life of running from school to baseball practice to my own classroom to soccer practice to research to piano lessons to committee meetings to swim meets had gradually wound down. I had to get used to it and I began to see emptiness as something completely different. It meant just less full.

Once a sense of stillness set in, I realized how grateful I was for having once had a home for myself and children. And again my thoughts turned to the women of the Grande'Anse who were overjoyed with each home that was built.

49
Closure

In the fall of 2010 a colleague asked if I would serve as keynote speaker for the local annual meeting of the American Association of University Women. They were interested in hearing about my work in Haiti. I hesitated for a number of reasons. First, I did not feel as if I had done anything remarkable, at least not worthy of a speech. Second, I had spoken to this group before. While the membership might have changed somewhat after these ten or more years, I feared the essence of the group remained the same and I had bombed with them the last time. I did not confess this to my colleague, hoping not to jar her memory in case she had been there. Third, I was not sure I would have anything wonderful to say. It was difficult to determine how much progress we were making on the UNOGA project or in Haiti in general. She assured me that whatever I could report would be much appreciated. In any case, the date of the luncheon was many months away and I could hardly tell her I had something else scheduled.

What made this particularly awkward was that university politics in the past had drawn battle lines between the two of us, and we were barely speaking to one another. The situation had been bad, and I came to distrust everyone in her court. I wondered what her motive was, and then admitted that an opportunity to speak about Haiti far superseded any personal issue at work. So, I said yes. By the time the date of the speaking engagement rolled around, my sensitivities regarding the earthquake had subsided and so, too, had my sensitivities regarding office tensions. This seemed a gesture of mending on her part, and for that I was grateful. An added appeal was that the luncheon was to be held at Innsbrook Country Club, where I had planned to speak when my father made his last trip to the hospital.

I arrived early, in order to place my feet firmly on the ground and get my bearings. Indiana's Saturdays in May can be the most beautiful days of the entire year, and this one was gorgeous. The walk up to the club house was lined with tulips and daffodils and the flowering trees were bursting with color. The golf course was as green as anything I had ever seen. I looked off into the distance trying to see where the houses of my father and his mother were situated. I scanned the horizon, imagining farmland. My grandmother once told me she was warned by her father that unpickled cucumbers would make her sick, so she would sneak out into the fields to eat them fresh. The farm must have reached for many acres because low-growing cucumber vines provide no place to hide. I liked thinking of her as a little girl. I also liked to think she told me that story as a loving acknowledgment that I did not always obey my father, her son, and it was ok.

Inside, I made small talk with the women in attendance. Some faces seemed familiar, but the atmosphere was not at all like what I had experienced before. It was not so much that they were more kind; rather, I was considerably less angry, or at least less unsure of the world and of myself. They appeared to be enthusiastically anticipating my talk. That fact did not make me more nervous, or less so, for talks are what they are.

Talks. It was simply my purpose to share experiences in Haiti, and describe the teaching project. Many of them were well-traveled and were curious about the country and its culture. Others could identify with the efforts of our post-secondary education program, I hoped, as they were university women themselves. There was really nothing for me to prepare, for I had reached a point where I could talk about Haiti for hours on end.

After reaching the microphone I hesitated for a moment and turned back to gaze through the wall of windows behind me. Smiling, I turned forward, and looked at my audience. The expanse of spring wrapped around my shoulders like a cloak of comfort.

"This used to be my great-grandfather's farm," I told them. "I've driven by many times, but never walked on the earth here before. My grandmother was born in a house down there on the highway and my father in the one near it." I paused for a moment and took a breath. "I'm happy to be here."

The talk went well and many questions followed. The energy was good. Life was good. Good things were happening in Haiti. Neither the situation nor the culture could have differed any more from what I knew of the Caribbean, but both worlds lived inside me.

CPSIA information can be obtained at www.ICGtesting.com
Printed in the USA
BVOW011927081112

305064BV00001B/1/P